The trans-Mississippi West of the nineteenth century held a singlar fascination for European visitors; they came in large numbers to satisfy their curiosity about the Red Indians, to hunt bison, or, particularly in the latter years of the century, to invest in cattle-raising or mining ventures. In this body of literature, apart from its intrinsic interest, the present volume holds a special place for two reasons: the overwhelming majority of the accounts were written by travelers from England, and Louis Laurent Simonin (1830–1886) was a Frenchman; moreover, he did not wait for the ceremonies at Promontory Point to visit the Rocky Mountain West. When he toured Colorado and Wyoming (then Dakota Territory) in the autumn of 1867, rail service extended only as far west as Julesburg.

Simonin, a mining engineer, visited the region at the invitation of the commissioner of Colorado Territory. Though the nation was rapidly expanding westward, the Plains Indians were still fighting to hold the lands that were their birthright, and Simonin witnessed the meeting of the Indian Peace Commission with Crow and Arapaho chiefs at Fort Laramie, in 1867. His report of the council, the only extant account by a civilian, acutely points up the issues involved in the "Indian question."

His descriptions of Denver, then a town of 8,000, the Colorado mining camps, and Cheyenne just before the railroad reached it have the freshness and immediacy of on-the-spot reporting—as indeed it was, for the book is made up of letters written to a friend in Paris. There are sketches in passing of New York and Chicago, and glimpses of such personalities as the fabulous promoter George Francis Train and Elizabeth Cady Stanton of suffragist fame.

The Rocky Mountain West in 1867

So far as can be determined, Wilson O. Clough's translation of this delightful, immensely readable account is the first to appear in English.

The translator. Professor of English and American studies, emeritus, at the University of Wyoming, DR. WILSON O. CLOUGH holds honorary degrees from Union College, Schenectady, N.Y. (Litt.D., 1957) and from the University of Wyoming (LL.D., 1961). He is the author of books, articles, short stories, poems, and reviews including, most recently, *Intellectual Origins of American National Thought* (1961) and *The Necessary Earth: Nature and Solitude in American Literature* (1964).

The Rocky Mountain West in 1867

by

LOUIS L. SIMONIN

Translated and annotated

by

WILSON O. CLOUGH

from

Le grand-ouest des Etats-Unis

UNIVERSITY OF NEBRASKA PRESS · LINCOLN

Earlier versions of portions of this translation have been previously published: part of Chapter 9 as "A French View of Cheyenne in 1867," *Frontier*, X (March 1930), 240–242; portions of Chapters 10 through 15 under the title "Fort Russell and the Fort Laramie Peace Commission in 1867," *Frontier*, XI (January 1931), 177–186, reprinted in State University of Montana, *Sources of Northwest History*, No. 14; and parts of Chapters 4 through 7 as "Colorado in 1867 as Seen by a Frenchman," *Colorado Magazine*, XIV (March 1937), 56–63.

Publishers on the Plains

UNP

F
594
. S613
1966

MANUFACTURED IN THE UNITED STATES OF AMERICA

Contents

List of Illustrations

vii

Translator's Foreword

The trans-Mississippi West of the nineteenth century held a singular fascination for European visitors; they came in large numbers to satisfy their curiosity about the Red Indians, to hunt the great bison, or, particularly in the latter years of the century, to invest in cattle-raising or mining ventures. Among the earliest who have left a record of their travels were Prince Maximilian von Wied-Neuwied, who toured the upper Missouri region in 1832, and Sir William Drummond Stewart, who visited the Rockies at about the same time. The real influx of travelers did not begin, however, until some twenty years later; and tourists were still something of a novelty until after the Civil War. After the completion of the transcontinental railroad in 1869, however, as Robert G. Athearn has written, "it was merely a matter of buying a railroad ticket if one wanted to have a look at much of the area. Since almost every part of the new land was available to the most cautious tourist, via the many branch lines, western America was literally overrun with travelers, most of whom, happily, had an insatiable urge to write of their observations."[1] In this body of literature the present volume, apart from its intrinsic interest, holds a special place for two reasons: the overwhelming majority of the accounts were written by travelers from England, and Louis Laurent Simonin (1830–1886) was a Frenchman; moreover, he did not wait for the ceremonies at Promontory Point to visit the Rocky Mountain West. When he toured the region in the autumn of 1867, rail service extended only as far west as Julesburg.

Born in Marseilles, Simonin was a mining engineer, a graduate of the School of Mines in St. Etienne, and after 1865 a professor of geology at the Ecole Centrale d'Architecture in Paris. An inveterate traveler, he had, prior to 1867, made scientific and exploratory trips to the mines of France and Italy, Madagascar, the island of Réunion, and in 1859, to California. He was a prolific writer; in addition to accounts of his travels

[1] Robert G. Athearn, *Westward the Briton* (Lincoln: University of Nebraska Press, 1962), p. 5.

he published a number of books dealing with geology and mining (see Selected Bibliography of Simonin's Writings, p. xiii), and contributed frequently to literary and scientific journals.

His 1867 trip, as Simonin tells us in his preface, followed on an invitation from J. P. Whitney, a commissioner from Colorado Territory to the Paris Exposition. A gentleman "largely engaged in the development of our mines," Whitney had, at his own expense, assembled a fine exhibit of minerals for the Exposition, and thereby "induced several eminent scientists of Europe to make exhaustive examinations of the gold, silver and other resources of the Territory, whose favorable reports, when published, caused the investment of foreign capital in them."[2] When Whitney returned to Colorado, he was accompanied by Simonin and Colonel Wilhelm Heine, then attaché to the American legation in Paris. Heine seems to have been a man of parts—a painter, writer, soldier, and traveler. Born in Dresden, he had studied art in Paris before emigrating to the United States in 1849 at the age of twenty-two. His travels took him to Central America and the Far East—he was a member of Commodore Perry's 1852 expedition to Japan. During the Civil War he saw action as a captain of engineers in the Union Army and later held the post of consul in Paris and Liverpool. The Whitney party arrived in Denver in early October.

In 1867 the United States was at the peak of a period of physical and industrial expansion, and Simonin was caught up in the prevailing sentiment that nothing could stop the tide of empire. Even the Civil War—which he mentions only in passing—appears to have been to him little more than an interruption in the steady drive westward. The mid-nineteenth century was indeed a watershed era, looking back to the difficulties of the early republic and ahead to the seemingly boundless promise of the future. Men still living remembered the Lewis and Clark expedition; mountain men and trappers were not yet a vanished breed; and the Colorado gold rush, the transcontinental telegraph, and the Pacific railroad were current news.

But underlying this frontier activity, so stimulating to Simonin, was the chronic Indian warfare which culminated during the decade

[2] Frank Hall, *History of the State of Colorado* (Chicago: Blakely, 1889–1895), I, 440–441.

of the sixties. With the withdrawal of government troops from the West during the Civil War, the hostile Plains Indians, in particular the Brulé Sioux, the Cheyennes, and the Arapahos, had become emboldened in their attacks on white settlements. The situation had become so critical that in 1866 travel in the Platte Valley came to a virtual standstill and work on the railroad was seriously threatened. While a majority of western sentiment favored a vindictive policy of reprisal—even mass extermination of the Indians if necessary—a small but vocal group, pointing to the deceit that had characterized the United States' dealings with the Indians and to the treaties the government had broken, called for a more conciliatory attitude. Congress entered the controversy by creating, in the summer of 1867, an Indian Peace Commission to treat with the warring chiefs in an effort to remove the causes of war, provide for the safety of frontier settlements, and inaugurate some plan for the civilization of the Indians.[3] Simonin was present at the meeting between the peace commissioners and Crow and Arapaho chiefs at Fort Laramie in November; and his report of the council, the only extant account by a civilian, acutely points up the issues involved in the "Indian question."

A practical man with an eye to the useful, Simonin finds much to admire in the Americans he met. The West in particular is to him an amazing phenomenon of productivity through freedom of enterprise, and he exhorts his European compatriots to learn from the example of the United States. Even his misgivings over the fate of the Indian do not go very deep, for it is his expressed opinion that progress is an inexorable master. Although he is no de Tocqueville, either for range of observation or for depth of analysis, Simonin writes with gusto and freshness, and his epistolary style—the book was originally written as letters to a friend in Paris—lends a sense of immediacy that enables us to share in his enthusiasm and excitement.

A NOTE ON THE TRANSLATION

The original title of the present volume, *Le grand-ouest des Etats-Unis*, has been altered for clarification. Simonin's description of his visit to

---

[3] James C. Olson, *Red Cloud and the Sioux Problem* (Lincoln: University of Nebraska Press, 1965), p. 58. See chapters 1–5 for a detailed account of the Plains Indian situation in the 1860's and of the councils of 1867 and 1868.

California in 1868, which comprised a supplement of some fifty pages subtitled "Pioneers of the Pacific" and was devoted primarily to technical descriptions of mining in California, has not been included in this translation.

The translation itself presented no great difficulties, for Simonin was without excessive literary flourishes. I have tried to render the text with accuracy, but without a stiff literalness. The spellings of proper names have been silently modernized; and a number of footnotes have been added, at the suggestion of the publisher, for the readers who may wish to be reminded of the setting for Simonin's work.

WILSON O. CLOUGH

Laramie,
Wyoming

Selected Bibliography of Simonin's Writings

Simonin's later books about the United States are more purely factual and statistical than the present volume; as noted below, one of them borrows from it and another was a reissue of previous writings.

A travers les Etats-Unis [*Across the United States*]. Paris, 1875.

l'Etrurie et les étrusques [*Etruria and the Etruscans*]. Paris, 1866.

Le grand-ouest des Etats-Unis [*The Great West of the United States: Pioneers and Redskins*]. Paris, 1869. Translated here under the title *The Rocky Mountain West in 1867*. Includes an account of Simonin's 1868 trip to California under the subtitle "Pioneers of the Pacific" omitted from this translation. *U.S.iana*, comp. Wright Howes (New York: Bowker, 1962), p. 531, erroneously states that this volume includes letters from Simonin's 1859 trip to California.

Histoire de la terre [*The History of the Earth: The Origin and Metamorphoses of the World*]. Paris, 1867.

l'Homme américain [*The American Man: Notes on the Indian*]. Paris, 1870. Report to the French minister of public instruction. Borrows from the present volume.

Les merveilles du monde souterrain [*Marvels of the Underground World*]. Paris, 1868

Les mineurs de Californie [*The Miners of California*]. Paris, 1866. Probably the same as the section on California in *Les pays lointains*.

Le monde américain: Souvenirs de mes voyages [*The American World: Memoirs of My Travels*]. Paris, 1876. Apparently a reissue of previous writings.

l'Or et l'argent [*Gold and Silver*]. Paris, 1877.

Les pays lointains [*Far-Away Lands: California, Maurice, Aden, Madagascar*]. Paris, 1867. Includes an account of Simonin's 1859 trip to California.

Les pierres [*Stones: Mineralogical Sketches*]. Paris, 1869.

Les ports de la Grande-Bretagne [*The Ports of Great Britain*]. Paris, 1881.

La richesse minérale de la France [*The Mineral Wealth of France*]. Paris, 1865.

La Toscane et la Mer Tyrrhénienne [*Tuscany and the Tyrrhenian Sea*]. Paris, 1868.

Une excursion chez les peaux rouges [*An Excursion Among the Redskins*]. Paris, 1868. Probably taken from *Le grand ouest*.

La vie souterraine [*Underground Life*]. 2d ed. Paris, 1867. Translated as *Underground Life: or Mines and Miners*, "Adapted to the present state of British Mining," London and New York, 1869.

The Rocky Mountain West in 1867

To my friend
Paul Dalloz

Author's Preface

The Exposition of 1867 brought to Paris, among other Americans, Mr. J. P. Whitney, an energetic Bostonian and commissioner of the territory of Colorado. We became acquainted, and Mr. Whitney proposed, as if it were the most natural thing in the world, that I come to visit his mines. Nor was this just a matter of undertaking a trip to the Champ de Mars, the site of the Exposition, but to the Rocky Mountains, some two thousand five hundred leagues from Paris, some six thousand miles. Mr. Whitney had come to the right person: I have always loved to travel, and I have made much greater journeys.

At that moment, however, it was neither the earth's surface nor its underground that I was investigating, but the atmosphere. I interrupted my aerial excursions and rejoined Mr. Whitney in America, along with a second companion, the gallant Colonel (later General) Heine, attaché to the American legation in Paris.

In the course of this voyage I wrote the following letters to a friend. I bring them together here in a volume. . . .[1]

I offer this little book to my compatriots in the hope that it will bring them to love, as I do, American freedom and democracy.

L. SIMONIN

Paris, June 1869

[1] Omitted here are a few sentences about the chapters on California, which do not appear in this translation.

3

CHAPTER 1

The Queen of the Lakes

Chicago, on Lake Michigan, 30 September 1867

All roads lead to Rome, it is said; all roads lead also to the Great American West. I took the shortest, the most direct, and hence I write my first letter two thousand leagues, nearly five thousand miles, from Paris, which I left but fifteen days ago.

On the evening of September 13, a Friday, I said my last farewell, as I pulled out of the Montparnasse station, to the palace and the garden of the Exposition, both of them brilliantly illuminated; and the following day I awoke in Brest. I embarked immediately on the *Saint-Laurent*, one of the finest steamers of the French transatlantic company, and one of the swiftest of its marvelous fleet. If you but realized how greatly our colors profit by being thus peacefully paraded upon the high seas!

With the help of fine weather and the vigilance of our captain, we made in nine days the distance of the more than 3,000 marine miles (1,400 leagues of four kilometres) that lie between Brest and New York. True, this was the *Saint-Laurent's* finest trip, but such voyages are quite the usual thing for the transatlantic company. The good Captain de Bocandé was quite delighted at this exceptional crossing, and I reflected that, as things were going, one might quite safely risk leaving on the 13th, even if it were also a Friday.

In New York I found once more my excellent traveling companion, Colonel Heine, attaché at the United States legation in Paris. He had preceded me by two weeks in order to prepare the itinerary of our great

4

excursion. He was ready, and I was equally so. I asked only a morning, to present my respects to our amiable consul general, M. the Baron Gauldrée Boilleau.

"So you want to go get yourself scalped in the Far West?" asked the Baron. "The Indians are always at war with the United States."

"I have promised to be there in the mines of Colorado."

"The Redskins will stop you in the desert, on the way from Julesburg to Denver."

"I have a good rifle and an excellent revolver."

"It is rather late now to undertake a geological expedition in the Rocky Mountains; you will find the mines under snow."

"Those words give me pause, coming from so reasonable and experienced a man as you. I'll reflect on it until tomorrow."

"Good-bye. And if you do go, come back with your hair."

I pondered for a few hours what the Baron had said, and the result of my meditations was that the weather was fine, that the Indian summer of the prairies, which corresponds to our Saint Martin's summer, was approaching under the most favorable auspices, and finally that if the Indians were destined to pierce me with arrows and scalp me, one died but once and not always by so dramatic an end, and I should not be the worst treated of the dying. So I cried, as the Americans do: "Go ahead! *En avant!*" The imperturbable Colonel accepted this motto of his adopted country, and on the evening of September 26, without further loss of time, we took our places for Omaha, or rather, produced for the railroad officials the tickets which the American railroad companies had freely put at our disposal, happy to be of service to travelers who went with such good grace to be scalped.

Omaha is situated on the Missouri, 1,500 miles from New York. Here I insert a paragraph to tell you, if you have no dictionary at hand, that the American mile, like the English, in round numbers equals 1,610 metres, and is therefore around two thirds longer than our official kilometre. Note, too, by the way, that the marine mile, which I mentioned above, is equal to 1,852 metres. There are miles and miles, as there are bundles and bundles, as Rabelais said.

From New York to Albany we followed the beautiful Hudson River. From Albany we pushed straight on to Lake Ontario, passing on the way cities like Troy, Ithaca, Rome, and Syracuse, whose names are designed to confuse the traveler if he is not wide awake. Fortunately, one also comes upon cities like Rochester, the big city of flour merchants, where the noise of wheels and mills, the bustle without pause or truce, reminds one that he is in the United States.

On the afternoon of the 27th we saluted the falls of Niagara, and crossed the river by the boldest, highest, and longest suspension bridge in the world; and so entered Canada and skirted all day the shores of Lake Erie.

At Detroit (a French name, like so many here, recalling our onetime domination in these parts), a "ferry boat" carried the whole train over the strait of water which links Lake Erie with Lake Huron, and we re-entered the United States in Michigan. Here begin the great plains of the Mississippi, the former prairies, the most beautiful habitation ever prepared by God for man, as Tocqueville, I believe it was, wrote.

On the morning of the 28th we arrived in Chicago. We were 1,000 miles from New York, covered in one stage, without fatigue, at a speed almost reaching that of our express trains. We had slept two nights in beds, in the coaches.[1] At evening the seats are transformed into small beds by a very ingenious process, and there one sleeps, I shall not say as well as at home, but certainly as well as in a steamer cabin. The beds are one above the other; and the only fear, if, like me, you have a huge companion sleeping over your head, is that you might receive him, luggage and all, full in your face, if just one spring was out of order; but I am told that this never happens.

The "palace cars" and "state rooms," which may be occupied alone, are even more comfortable, and certainly too luxurious for a country so democratic. Never a sovereign traveled in so much comfort as in these reserved compartments, which may be got on all the large American railroads for a few dollars.

These sleeping compartments are called "sleeping cars," as you might say dormitory rooms or bedrooms. You know that the American cars are large, high, well aired, capable of accommodating some fifty travelers. The seats are arranged in rows, with an aisle contrived in

---

[1] The first true Pullman sleeping car dated from 1859, on the run from Chicago to Bloomington, Illinois.

6

between. You may ride as you wish, forward or backwards, for the seat may be swung around a lateral pivot.

In each compartment is a pitcher of water and a drinking glass, a basin, and a stove which may be heated in winter; and finally, must I say it? a "water closet," so badly needed in our trains. A cord extending the whole length of the train puts each compartment in contact with the engineer. One may pass at will from one car to another while the train is in motion, and even stand outside, leaning on the railing to admire the country at one's ease.

An employee passes through each car selling newspapers, books, fruits, and eatables, and from time to time the conductor of the train verifies the tickets without disturbing you, because each takes care to place his ticket in the ribbon of his hat. But, you will say, we know all that; it is not necessary to repeat it for us. To which I reply that our railroads in France are still so little comfortable that we cannot too often recall that the Americans surpass us here and do much better than we.

Smoking is permitted in certain compartments only; but everywhere tobacco is chewed, and you know how the Americans are—chewers. The ladies, for whom everyone here has the greatest respect, may be incommoded by these habits; hence you find reserved carriages on all trains. Husbands and others who without the title accompany the ladies may enter the compartment, as I have frequently longed to do. The "bachelor," not, as you might suppose, a bachelor of arts, but a man without a wife, enjoys no standing in the United States. The English minister, Sir Frederick Bruce,[2] who died just a few days since in Boston, and who was not married (there are such ministers), always took his cook with him on his travels. With this "lady" he went everywhere; all reserved doors were open to him, and he thus escaped the often barely tolerable company of the American smokers and chewers. As to the servant, she followed her master as if she were his wife: there is no barrier of rank in the United States.

I said that we were in Chicago, recently named the Queen of the Prairies. It is the marvel of the West, the queen of the lakes, as it is also

[2] Sir Frederick Bruce (1814–1867) held major posts as a British diplomat in Washington (1842), Hong Kong, Newfoundland, Bolivia and Uruguay, Egypt, China, and again in Washington (1865).

7

called, for the prairies are now quite distant. It is the one city among all that visitors to the United States must see.

"Visit two things only in America," said an English statesman who was leaving for New York, "Niagara Falls and Chicago." He was right. If the Niagara Falls are the most astonishing in the world, Chicago is also the most marvelous city ever built by man. In 1830 it had but seventy inhabitants. At that time there was but a military fort, erected against the Indians, and a trading post, built by the Astors of New York for their commerce in furs there.[3] Today Chicago comprises 225,000 inhabitants, and its population increases every day. It is the greatest grain market of the entire world, and leaves Odessa, Trieste, and Marseille far behind. It is one of the most beautiful cities of the United States.

The hotel where we stopped, the Sherman House, can lodge a thousand travelers.[4] It is built entirely of white marble, "Athens marble," as the Americans say. There are several hotels of equal importance in Chicago. That is not the sole object of interest in the city. The "elevators," where grains are mechanically prepared as they arrive by railroad and leave by ship, also deserve to be seen. The grain is lifted, winnowed, purified, classified, taken on trains, and loaded on ships, all by means of machinery, without the buyer or seller's being in the least involved, or even seeing his merchandise.

The means of supplying drinking water from Lake Michigan is also one of the marvels of this city, and this under-lake tunnel, two miles long, is more remarkable even than that of London under the Thames. You surely recall the miracles of building construction done here, the raising of houses several metres above their natural level when it became necessary to raise the original level of the city. The houses were supported

---

[3] The first real survey for Chicago was in 1830. By 1844 Chicago claimed eighteen hotels and public houses. See Bessie L. Pierce, *A History of Chicago* (New York: Knopf, 1937), and Edgar Lee Masters, *The Tale of Chicago* (New York: G. P. Putnam's, 1933).

[4] The Sherman House, originally built in 1836 and remodeled in 1844, was torn down for the one which M. Simonin visited, "the largest and most splendid hotel in Illinois," from its own advertisement. It boasted seven stories and an observatory on the roof from which its proprietor could see the approach of steamboats and have his carriages in waiting. This building burned in 1871 and was rebuilt the following year.

at the four corners by jackscrews or spiral screws, then a row of these tools was set up along the whole length and width of the buildings. A winch was turned, and in a few days the thing was done. The inhabitants had not even left their houses. This method deserves to be recommended to M. Haussmann,[5] and a plan of it may be seen in the palace of the Exposition. "Give me a lever," said Archimedes, "and I will move the earth." The lever here is the jackscrew and the spiral screw, cousins-german of the lever, mechanisms powerful because they are slow. What is gained in power is lost in speed—you know the mechanical principle as it was taught to us at the lycée.

Chicago is situated on Lake Michigan, as Marseille is on the Mediterranean. From its inland sea and by way of its Erie and Welland canals, Chicago can send its ships even to the Atlantic *without breaking bulk*, that is to say, without shifting cargo. They descend the Saint Lawrence after clearing the canals and lakes. Ships have gone thus, they say, from Lake Michigan to Liverpool and return. Not satisfied with that, the Americans talk of rushing a canal from Chicago to New York. Nothing is impossible for these people.

Aside from grains (wheat, maize, oats, etc.), sent from the vast plains watered by the Mississippi by the seventeen railroads radiating out from the city, Chicago also exports lead from the great foundries of Wisconsin and Illinois, coal, poured out by all the neighboring coal mines, and wood, furnished in considerable quantities by the nearby forests and retailed in planks and *houses*. The cities which spring up so rapidly every day in the United States send all their orders to Chicago. Chicago also exports skins, furs, and cattle in quantity, competing with Cincinnati and disputing with it the nickname of Porcopolis, the city of porkers.

Do not be alarmed, you do not meet these interesting animals anywhere in the streets. They do not obstruct circulation any more than the grains.

As in Cincinnati, the pig, after being fattened in the country, is mechanically cut up in the city into hams and lard; even the bristles are

---

[5] Baron George Eugène Haussmann was an engineer and *préfet* of the Seine (1853–1870) who planned much of nineteenth-century Paris—its buildings, streets, and parks—on a grandiose scale.

utilized. The animals come in single file by a passageway, a trap door opens, they fall through it one by one and are suffocated in a vat of boiling water. A sharp knife, moved by steam, opens them, cuts them up, divides them. In brief, the hams salt themselves and stack themselves in barrels. When they lack the required weight, they refuse to take their place on the pile. You know M. Devinck's clever machine to manufacture, weigh, wrap, and stack chocolate bars, the joy of visitors at all the expositions. Well, at Porcopolis, hams are manufactured, weighed, and stacked in the same way. Agree with me that this machine is missing from our great exposition on the Champ de Mars.

A "lecturer," as he is called here because he often reads his discourse —one means of not getting caught short—one day unfolded before the Chicagoans all the marvels of their city. When he came to the subject of pigs, he computed, like a true American economist, the quantity of corn needed to fatten these noble beasts, and the number of hams from each pig, and such and such a quantity of hams sent to England. "It is as if a fleet of so many ships," he cried, "loaded with corn, descended the Saint Lawrence, and as if an army of so many pigs crossed the Atlantic by swimming and came to a halt at London!" He was covered with applause.

How better could I conclude these few lines on Chicago?

CHAPTER 2

The Missouri

Omaha, on the Missouri, 1 October

Before the mysterious plains of the Great West lie spread ahead of me, I pause a second time and forward a souvenir of Omaha, on the right bank of the Missouri. Civilization, life with European customs, lies on this side of the stream—or river, if you prefer, for the Mississippi above St. Louis receives the waters of the Missouri, of a much greater length than its own. Beyond is the unknown, the life nomadic, the country of the Redskins, the "Far West," whose boundaries retreat every day before the ever more rapid march of the pioneer.

Already the Missouri no longer marks the line where the American desert begins. Omaha, on the right bank, is a pretty city, agreeably situated on the hills which mark the banks of the Missouri and peopled by 15,000 inhabitants. It has elegant houses, imposing buildings.[1]

It is at the same time the head of the Pacific railroad which marches toward the Rocky Mountains, only just now being reached. Then the iron road enters the country of the Mormons, in what Humbolt and Fremont called the great basin or inland basin because there the waters have no drainage toward the ocean, but instead into salt lakes

[1] The site of Omaha was an early stopping place for traders and trappers. The first settlement began in 1846–1847, when the Mormons passed through on their way to Utah. However, it was not until 1854, with the passage of the Kansas-Nebraska Act, that "Omaha City" was formally organized. See James C. Olson, *History of Nebraska* (Lincoln: University of Nebraska Press, 1955), pp. 83–85.

11

or inland seas. Nevertheless, another railroad, starting from Sacramento, in California, crosses the state of Nevada to the very rich silver mines, and from there advances toward the first portion. Within three years, perhaps two, a continuous ribbon of iron will link the two oceans, Atlantic and Pacific. Omaha has been among the first to profit by the advantages of this railroad. It had 3,000 inhabitants in 1862, when this great project was approved; today it has 15,000.

We came by railroad from Chicago to Omaha, crossing the fertile plains of Illinois, the state in which Lincoln was born,[2] and across Iowa, only yesterday frequented by the trappers of Canada, today decisively occupied by American farmers. Underground riches supplement those of the soil, and along the way we came on several coal mines actively exploited.

In twenty-four hours we crossed the 500 miles which separated us from Omaha, sleeping the best of travelers' slumbers at night in the "sleeping cars." We had a new companion, Mr. Whitney, commissioner from Colorado at the World Exposition on the Champ de Mars, where he received a gold medal. The grand prize was awarded the miners of that rich territory. Mr. Whitney will be our guide to the gold and silver mines of Colorado.

Our coach was occupied almost solely by emigrants, colonists, pioneers, men of the Far West, as they are called. We differed from all those folk by our appearance, habits, language, even type. The American talks freely while traveling. We were asked who we were, where we were going. Mr. Whitney spoke softly of Colonel Heine as the Pope of the Mormons, Brigham Young; he and I, he said, were neophytes in the new church, recently converted Latter Day Saints. The news spread swiftly from mouth to mouth. The ladies looked with a gratified eye on this high priest of Salt Lake, this husband of thirty-two wives, and some seemed even willing to join him. A farmer from Kansas, returning to his country, presented his notebook to the false Brigham Young for his inscription; but the prophet declined the honor so as not to arouse jealousy. If he satisfied a single one of such requests he would have to do so for all, and this would be truly too many autographs to give out.

[2] An obvious error, but understandable on Simonin's part, since Lincoln was generally associated with Illinois, rather than Kentucky, where he was born.

The Missouri

A young lady approached me and with a familiar manner opened a conversation. "Is your friend really the head of the Mormons?"

"He is indeed. Brigham Young never lies."

"He must be really happy to have so many wives!"

"One never has too many. What is lacking in one he finds in another."

"He is very polite and civilized."

"Do you think Mormons are ogres? Polygamy can only soften manners."

"Where are you going?"

"To Colorado, to visit the gold and silver mines and to make some converts on the way. Shall we be stopped by Indians?"

"I don't think so. I am going to Colorado, too, to find my brother in Denver. They say the Indians recently stopped the stagecoach; but I hope they won't do it this time, and that we won't be scalped."

This woman's calm courage was such as to give heart to the most timid, and I reflected that I had been decidedly right to make the journey by stages in the Great West and feel out the land before me. More than ever I said, "*En avant*, go ahead!"

As we passed from the state of Illinois to Iowa we crossed the Mississippi on a long wooden bridge with swinging girders. From the Mississippi to the Missouri we ran over a double ribbon of iron which extended straight before us, and whose extremities seemed to meet on the horizon. The graders had not much to do in the midst of these vast plains to prepare the soil for the track.

Council Bluffs was our last station on the left bank of the Missouri, and there a steam ferry received travelers and vehicles alike and deposited them on the opposite bank.[3]

The river is wide; but its waters are shallow and muddy, yellow as those of the Tiber, the *flavum Tiberim* of which Horace sang. The "bluffs" or knolls of clay and friable sandstone which line either bank are little by little undercut by the current and imperceptibly descend into the river. The trees which crown the bluffs fall with them, so that the current is often blocked by these natural rafts, which create a considerable obstacle to navigation, since they are most of the time hidden

[3] Transportation from Council Bluffs to Omaha was by ferry until a bridge was constructed in 1872.

13

at the bottom of the stream. This phenomenon takes place on a still larger scale on the Mississippi; there, there are not only rafts but even floating islands. You are aware that certain geologists have called on this fact to explain the deposits of fossil coal, and that often cited are the forests carried by the Mississippi and deposited toward its delta, there to be heaped up in the river's silt, as a phenomenon which could account for a carboniferous sediment. This is an excellent method often pursued by geologists in the effort to explain past phenomena by present causes, but this is not the time to prolong a discussion which would lead too far afield; I return to my topic, Omaha.

For a long time here the muddy waters of the stream sufficed for all domestic needs. It is said that travelers passing through used to grow red with rage, asking who had washed before them in the basin, or even if it was the custom in Omaha to pour dirty water into the water pitcher. Others, coming from the bath, muttered between their teeth the verse which Martial exploded on an attendant at the Baths of Rome, as he paid his tip: "*Ubi lavantur qui hic lavantur?* Where shall they bathe who have bathed here?"

Today all this is changed: Omaha has clear water or filters it from the Missouri. The city must be worthy of the title of head of the Pacific railroad.

This is a strange country, this Great American West. Little by little the pioneers conquer the land of the Redskin, and Omaha even owes its name to the Indians of the Omaha tribe, who but recently camped on the very spot on which the city is built. Where are the Omahas today? Impounded in some "reservation" imposed on them by the whites. There they slowly die of smallpox, drunkenness provoked by "fire water," the whiskey which they so misuse, and other more deplorable maladies. This is the way so many tribes have disappeared, and the way they will all disappear.

War, too, has greatly aided in the extermination of the Redskin. Where are the Hurons, the Iroquois, the Natchez, who so astounded our fathers? The Algonquins, who did not even know the limits of their powerful empire, where and how many of them are there now?

I met only a few Pawnees in Omaha, those ruthless enemies of the Sioux. Today they are on a reservation in the territory of Nebraska, in the vicinity of the Pacific railroad.[4] They come often to Omaha to buy provisions and clothing. They saunter along the streets in groups of two or three. A blanket of wool or a buffalo robe thrown over the back sometimes composes all their clothing. Trousers, the particular mark of civilized nations, seem to inconvenience them, and they commonly scalp them, that is, rid them of the seat; they seem thus more comfortable to wear. On their feet they wear moccasins or sandals of leather decorated with designs; around the neck a collar of beads or glass trinkets; in the hair, if they have the right to the title of chief, an eagle feather or—a chicken's. They customarily carry with them the quiver, bow and arrows, and often the calumet, a pipe with a long stem decorated with brass nails and a bowl of red earth.

I bought from one of these Indians a bow, also his arrows and his very fine quiver, made from the skin of a young buffalo. The arrow points are of sharpened iron, triangular, not poisoned. The shaft is fitted at the other end with barbs of feathers. In several spots traces of blood are visible; I imagine that it is nothing but buffalo blood. The arrow has been recovered from the animal killed in the hunt, a quite understandable economy.

The same Indian agreed to sell me his necklace of beads, of a curious design. I got the whole for eight dollars (around forty francs), paid, it is true, in "green-backs," or paper money, the only money in circulation since the war in the United States, which at this moment loses forty per cent in exchange for gold.

The Pawnees, like all prairie Indians, have oval faces; black hair, long and stiff; an aquiline nose; a thin-lipped mouth; and delicate extremities of arms and feet; often prominent cheekbones; and eyes slightly narrowed. Their glance is fixed, melancholy. The skin is tanned, somewhat reddish. They are evidently of a special race, whether indigenous or emigrated, a red or copper race. But this is not the place for ethnological digressions. Besides, who will discover the truth about them, and would not the report still be in doubt?

[4] The Pawnees once occupied central Nebraska, north and south of the Platte River. In 1833 they ceded all their lands south of the river to the United States government. In 1848 they sold a strip along the north bank of the Platte between present-day Grand Island and Kearney, Nebraska; and in 1857 they ceded all their lands north of the Platte, except a 450-square-mile tract on the Loup River which was set aside as a reservation. (Olson, *History of Nebraska*, p. 83.)

The territories of Nebraska and Kansas, the latter bordering on the south, are not occupied solely by subdued Indians, like the Pawnees and Omahas. The indomitable Cheyennes, the terrible Arapahos, the bloody Sioux, have many times, and even recently, spread terror on these plains.[5]

Scarcely two months ago some employees of the Pacific railroad who had gone out to repair the telegraph poles along the track were surprised by a band of Indians and pitilessly massacred. A single victim, an Englishman, M. W. T——, survived. Struck down by a bullet, beaten by a blow of the rifle, stabbed by a knife, he fell unconscious. The Indian who attacked him took him for dead and scalped him. As he mounted his horse, the Redskin dropped his trophy. M. W. T. regained his consciousness, retrieved his scalp, and returned to Omaha, where his companions had been solemnly buried. Our Paris journals published this story early in September, but one could hardly believe that a man scalped alive had been able to survive so horrible an operation and to tell of his own martyrdom. I took it for a tall tale, a "humbug." The fact is verified and must be taken for true: M. W. T. is still in Omaha. Furthermore, it appears that his is not the only case of a man scalped alive. The wound healed over quickly; nevertheless, there remains a hideous tonsure, and such a man is obliged to wear a wig: he had better start with that.

The rebellious Redskins do not stop with killing and scalping whites in this country; they have twice attacked trains on the Pacific railroad, derailed them, and taken the engineer and his helpers by surprise.

The Redskins have no love for the civilization that advances through the prairies and scatters the buffalo, the sole source of existence for the children of the desert. What if we should be surrounded by Indians on the train that takes us from Omaha to Julesburg, or on the coach which will transport us from Julesburg to Denver! "Never mind," there

[5] The Cheyennes and northern Arapahos lived at this period chiefly between the north and south forks of the Platte River and eastward. The Sioux tribe encompassed a number of divisions and bands. Those whom Simonin encountered were subdivisions of the Teton group, namely, the Blackfeet, who roamed over the Montana country; the Brulés, who ranged south of the Black Hills; and the Oglalas, also in the Black Hills area and in eastern Wyoming. See T. A. Larson, *A History of Wyoming* (Lincoln: University of Nebraska Press, 1965), Chapter II.

16

is now no time to retreat. There are still these two stages of our journey before we arrive in Colorado, and these we must undertake, cost what it may. My next letter will be dated therefore from Julesburg, on the Platte River,[6] which is at the moment the last station on the Pacific railroad. I shall write further, God willing, about this railroad, one of the marvels of our time.

[6] Simonin consistently spells the name of this river *Plate*. For his reasons for doing so, see below, page 20.

CHAPTER 3

The Tall Grass Country

Julesburg, on the Platte River, 2 October

I have finally reached the terminus of this railroad of the Pacific, this railroad born yesterday, which will in a few years be the great artery of the commercial world. I have covered a distance of 380 miles, between Omaha and Julesburg, between the head of the line on the Missouri and the point which is for the moment the last stop toward the Rocky Mountains. All honor to the martyr president who in 1862 authorized the route with the same pen which was later to sign the abolition of slavery! Up to that point the jealous opposition of the southern states had alone prevented the opening of this railroad which the Americans had dreamed of for years, especially since the acquisition of California in 1848.[1]

The grade had been leveled by nature, and we rolled the whole distance across a prairie as level as an alluvial sea. The tall grass, in summer growing often as high as a man, was already yellow; and here and there a few poor flowers raised their heads amid the sod, the last gems of the rich jewelry of springtime. Here finally was the prairie which every

---

[1] President Lincoln had in 1863 designated Omaha as the eastern terminus of the Union Pacific railroad; and in California the Central Pacific had just previously been chartered, to be built from Sacramento eastward to meet the Union Pacific. As early as the 1840's there had been agitation in Congress for the establishment of a transcontinental railroad, but northerners and southerners were unable to agree upon a choice of routes. After the outbreak of the Civil War, southern opposition was eliminated, and Congress was able to authorize the railroad.

18

traveler burns to see in America, and which I was quite happy to have reached without difficulties.

That night, stretched out on one of the beds of the sleeping car, found even at this distance, I slept with but one eye. I dreamed of Indians, and it seemed to me several times, when the train stopped (as the word is), that it was they who had held up the locomotive.

On one occasion the Colonel called to me to show me the prairie on fire. I thought it was a false alarm and put my hand on my revolver. The fire extended over an immense space and was reflected in the sky itself. Some passerby, an Indian, had set fire to the first bunch of grass by chance or by design, or perhaps a spark had escaped from the locomotive. The flames had spread gradually across the dry turf. All through the autumn, great black stains mark the spots which have been so burned. In spring the grass pushes up even sturdier and higher.

The stations we passed have a name, but as yet for the most part no inhabitants. While with us we build a railroad only toward populous locations, here the Americans in inverse fashion throw a railroad across the prairie desert in order to attract the settler as soon as possible.

Read the names of these germs of future cities, the embryos of cities which will one day be so great. They are, as one leaves Omaha, Fremont, dedicated to the celebrated explorer who was among the first to cover this vast American territory from Atlantic to Pacific; Columbus, tardy justice given to Columbus; Kearney, close to the fort of the same name, the favored station of the buffalo, or rather the bison, savage bull of the prairies.[2] Farther along is Plum Creek, a name which awakens sad memories for the hunters of the plains; for it was here that the Indians recently committed one of the worst of their depredations, and only

---

[2] Fremont, a station for western immigrants from 1856 on, was named for John Charles Fremont, who in 1844 suggested the name of Nebraska, an Indian word for the Platte River. Columbus, likewise dating from 1856 as a supply point for wagon trains, had been moved from its original site to a location on the Union Pacific. The town of Kearney, named in honor of General Stephen Watts Kearny, was incorporated in 1860. Fort Kearny, established as a military post in 1848, was also named for Stephen Watts Kearny. See Lilian L. Fitzpatrick, *Nebraska Place-Names* (Lincoln: University of Nebraska Press, 1960), pp. 25, 54, 115.

two months ago killed and scalped the persons I mentioned in my previous letter.[3]

North Platte, near Fort McPherson, is an important station. Here the Platte, or Nebraska, River, which we have followed from Omaha, divides into two branches: the North Platte, which comes from Fort Laramie; the South Platte, which comes from Denver, the metropolis of Colorado.[4]

From the North Platte to Julesburg we run along the side of the South Platte. At North Platte in the morning, we crossed the river on a magnificent wooden bridge. The air is pure, transparent, the sky blue, without a cloud. I am told that this is the kind of weather we shall enjoy for a month; a happy good fortune for a Parisian who so rarely sees the sun. True, we have gaslight over there, and can give it the name the Indians give the moon: the sun of night. Gas is still unknown on the prairies; but there is the sun by day and the moon by night, when it is its turn to show itself.

I said that from Omaha to Julesburg we ran along the Platte. The railroad holds to the left bank; it might equally well have chosen the right, for the prairie is naturally level on either side, and the Platte, with its low banks and its broad and shallow waters, well deserves its name.

I spell this name as it is spelled in French, *Plate*, and for a purpose, though the Americans have always written it with two *t*'s. That is not good orthography. The country is full of French names conferred on it by our former trappers, Canadians and Louisianians, who were the first to rove, and still rove, the prairies, from south to north, from east to west, hunting the buffalo, tending their beaver traps, and carrying on a barter exchange with the Indians, *trade*, from whence the name "traders" still given these rovers of the great plains. They baptized many

---

[3] Plum Creek, an early Pony Express station and trading post on the Platte River across from the site of present Lexington, Nebraska, was the scene of massacres in 1864, by Sioux and Cheyennes, and 1867, when the Cheyennes wrecked trains and scalped the crews.

[4] Fort McPherson, established in 1863, was about eighteen miles southeast of North Platte. The town of North Platte was laid out in 1866 in anticipation of the coming of the railroad. Here the railroad, which had thus far followed the route of the old Oregon Trail, turned south along the South Platte River, while the Oregon Trail continued along the North Platte.

another place besides the Platte. Prairie du Chien; the Des Moines River in Iowa; the Mauvaises Terres [Bad Lands] in Nebraska; Laramie fort, peak, and river in Dakota; the Bijou stream; the Cache à la Poudre; the Fontaine qui Bout [Boiling Spring]; La Porte pass, in Colorado, are all French names, respected by the Americans and found on all the maps. The very word "prairie," given to the great plains of the Far West, was borrowed from our language. The same is true of the names of many Indian tribes: the Brûlés [burned]; the Gros Ventres [big bellies]; the Pieds Noirs [Blackfeet]; the Corbeaux [Crows]; the Têtes Plates [Flathead]; the Nez Percés [pierced noses]; the Coeurs d'Alène [hearts of the awl, indicating sharpness in trading]; the Sans Arcs [without bows]; the Serpents [Snakes]; the Chiens [dogs], from which the Cheyennes[5]; the Santés [healthy], etc., all these names are of French origin and accepted by all American geographers.

Of all our former dominance in these areas, this is all that remains. The Louisianians and Canadians continue in their occupation as trappers and traders, but the latter have passed under English control and the former have become American citizens. France sends no more colonizers to the prairies; she has lost all possessions in America since the shameful reign of Louis XIV. The language alone has been retained, with a number of archaisms which continue to enchant all our old professors.[6]

Travel by train is too swift when one is crossing picturesque country; then the tourist curses the speed and would willingly prefer the old stagecoach, voyaging comfortably, watching the landscape unroll little by little. But on the prairie, since the landscape is monotonous and always horizontal, train travel is more appropriate. From North Platte to Julesburg, all the natural grasses, families, species, varieties, pass in a few hours before one's eyes; also the fragrant plants of the desert, sage, artemisia, the everlasting flower, and certain dwarf cacti. Trees

[5] Simonin here repeats an early confusion, found in Lewis and Clark, of the French "*chien*" (dog) with "Cheyenne." The word "Cheyenne" in actuality comes from the Sioux and means "people of alien speech." (Frederick Webb Hodge, ed., *Handbook of American Indians North of Mexico* [New York: Pageant Books, 1959], I, 250.)

[6] A reference, of course, to the Canadian French, which still retains vestiges of sixteenth- and seventeenth-century French.

are scarce, and only rarely does one encounter along the streams certain poplars, one species of which, the Canadian poplar (*populus monilifera*), here bears the name of *cottonwood*, doubtless because the leaves are covered underneath with a white cottony fuzz. The cottonwood is especially dear to the plains hunter and gladly sighted, since, like the palm of the African oasis, it is the tree which announces the presence of water.

Clumps of the river birch mingle with the cottonwood along the streams, a wood valued by those crossing the prairie by wagon train for starting the campfires for the night.

The fauna of the great American desert is no more varied than the flora. Everywhere are the buffalo, or bison, enormous bulls with great heads and thick pelt. The Indian hunts the buffalo for food and for hides to tan. The hide, or "robe," serves as a coat or covering for the Redskin, and forms the principal object of commerce with the whites. The tanned hide is used to cover his tent; the flesh, drawn out into narrow strips like straps and dried in the sun, lasts indefinitely. The smoked tongue, a delicate morsel, is the only part which the whites willingly eat.

The Indians make spoons and powder horns from the horns of the buffalo; from the bones they make scratching knives, scrapers, to scrape the hides which they tan with the brains of the animal; from the tendons of the muscles they make cords and a lining for their bows, and with the gelatine from the hoofs a glue to hold the points of their arrows. The Indian thus finds everything in the buffalo, beginning with his chief diversion, hunting. So he follows it in all his migrations; and there is a saying on the prairies: Where the buffalo is, there is the Indian. The Redskin adds further that a tradition runs through all the tribes, namely, that there will be no more Indians when the day arrives that there are no more buffalo. As in so many other places, primitive man will disappear with the primitive animal. For this reason the Redskin is so hostile to civilization, which, invading the prairies, disperses the buffalo in all directions and little by little brings about his own disappearance.

Along with the buffalo as the principal animals of the great plains are the beaver, which build their clever dams along the streams, and the

22

prairie dogs, not too unlike the marmot, the cony, and the squirrel, which live in a republic of underground villages covering immense areas. We must add the prairie wolf, or coyote, an ever hungry meat eater, and the graceful antelope, herds of which go by as swiftly as the wind. The antelope lives, like the buffalo, on the grasses of the desert; turf is nowhere lacking, and the prairie has rightly been named the terrestrial paradise of animals.

As one approaches the mountains, the fauna changes, or rather increases, into new species. There the deer, elk, hart, bear, and wildcat give the resolute hunter something to exercise his skill on.

This digression on the zoology and botany of the Great West has taken me away from Julesburg.[7] I return. This improvised city is at the moment the last railroad station of the Pacific, a title which it will very soon yield to Cheyenne, 140 miles to the west and soon to be reached. The iron path advances swiftly here. Originally the land belonged to no one, then nature took care to level it off and give it a gentle ascent, better than the most skilled of engineers could have done. Thus the grade is gradually prepared from the Missouri to the Rocky Mountains, and up to several kilometres of railroad can be laid daily. Everybody moves west with the railroad; the very inhabitants of Julesburg will little by little abandon that city for Cheyenne.

Only recently it was the railroad which advanced where there were no cities; now the cities precede the iron path, establishing themselves in the midst of the desert and saying to the railroad, "Come to us!" The mysterious advance of the human race, since earliest times in history, has always pushed westward; but has it ever been witnessed in a livelier and more striking fashion? Indeed, there is a whole new era revealed in this great labor of the United States, at the very hour when we are discussing the piercing of the Isthmus of Panama. It is the ribbon of iron in our era which will pierce isthmuses; in two years, the iron path of the Pacific will carry those who wish to tour the world in three

[7] The original Julesburg, named for Jules Beni, a French-Canadian trader, was an Overland stage and Pony Express station located a few miles south of the present Julesburg. It was attacked in 1862 and destroyed by Indians in 1865. A third site was established on the railroad in 1867, and the town was moved to the present site on the Union Pacific cutoff to Denver in 1881.

months.[8] Asia will come to visit Europe, and Europe, Asia by this great commercial route, by way of what has so well been called the center of gravity of the United States.

From Paris one will visit Japan or China in thirty or forty days by the shortest route, straying very little from the great circle of the terrestrial globe. Two steamboat lines and one railroad, and the thing is done. Le Havre or Brest, New York, San Francisco, such will be the major stops of the journey. But while we await the completion of such a project, let us return to our own more modest one.

Julesburg, where we are, is defended by Fort Sedgwick. We have just visited the fort, where Colonel Heine has discovered several companions in arms, among them General Potter, commandant of the place.[9] The General has had his young wife and children brought in. It takes a certain courage to exile oneself thus in the heart of the desert, but American women do not bargain over their devotion, and besides are great travelers.

Certain Indians are camped around the fort, Sioux, of the Oglala and Brulé bands. One sees their conical tents rising in the midst of the prairie. Red Cloud and Spotted Tail[10] have come with their men to treat with the commissioners of the Union. Peaceful today, these bands may perhaps tomorrow take up again their terrible chant of war.

A few years ago Fort Sedgwick was surrounded by Cheyennes, Sioux, and Arapahos in league against the whites, during the time of the War of Secession. The Redskins had forgotten for the time their former intestine wars, and turned their efforts against the common enemy.

---

[8] A railroad had been completed across the Isthmus of Panama in 1855; the canal, however, was not completed until many years later. Jules Verne's *Around the World in Eighty Days*, which described the Pacific railroad, appeared in 1872.

[9] Fort Sedgwick, about ten miles south of Julesburg, was built as a military post in 1864. General Joseph Haydn Potter (1822–1892), a classmate of Ulysses S. Grant at West Point, had fought in the Mexican War, accompanied the Utah expedition in 1857–1858, and was wounded in the Civil War at Chancellorsville. He held various posts in the West after 1866.

[10] Red Cloud (1822–1909), an important Oglala chief and leader of the band of Bad Faces, had since 1865 led the opposition to the building of the Bozeman Trail through Sioux country to the gold fields of Montana and was a leader in the 1866 attack on Fort Phil Kearny in Wyoming and the Fetterman massacre. Spotted Tail (*ca.* 1833–1881) was a Brulé chief. Simonin gives these chiefs the names of Nuée Rouge and Queue Bariolée.

Emigrants, pioneers, fleeing in fright, took refuge in the fort. The prairies had been set on fire all around. The Indians, to the number of several thousand, threatened to subdue the besieged by hunger. The attackers could be repulsed only by cannon and grapeshot.

But I must leave Julesburg; I hear the continental stage just arriving, the "overland mail."

We have one portion of our journey yet to make, my companions and I, a stretch of 190 miles across the great desert. We have with us an escort of six soldiers, perched on our vehicle, from where they survey the terrain. I shall write you from Denver if we arrive safe and sound, or if we are scalped en route by the Cheyennes and Arapahos, whose territory we cross, and have to buy a wig to adorn our occiput.

CHAPTER 4

The Transcontinental Stage

Fortune favors the bold. Here we are, having arrived without any unpleasant encounters during the trials of the journey. It was time. Sioux, Arapahos and Cheyennes were beginning to run through my head and make me lose sleep.

We left Julesburg on the evening of the second, and entered Denver yesterday toward midnight. Thirty hours by coach, 190 miles of travel, such is the active and passive of this last stage of our journey.

The stage which brought us is called the "overland mail," or transcontinental stage, because it crosses the whole continent from Julesburg on the Platte to Sacramento in California. Letters and travelers often take this route in place of the sea voyage and the Isthmus of Panama.

Before the opening of the Pacific railroad, the land mail went from Missouri to California, leaving and arriving at a fixed hour, a distance of some 800 leagues, or some 1,900 miles. The trip took twenty days. Never in the days of ancient history did the couriers of the Caesars or the Mogul princes, or in our own day those of the emperors of Russia, cross such great distances with such speed.[1]

Shall I give you a description of the vehicle which brought us here, and which, leaving us at Denver, continued its journey on into the

[1] Overland Mail coaches boasted as much as 110–115 miles a day, comparable to Simonin's figures. Benjamin Holladay's daily stage had from 1861 on claimed as much as 160 miles a day.

Rocky Mountains, the Mormon country, the state of Nevada, and the placer mines of Eldorado?

Imagine a kind of Louis XIV coach, for American carriages have not changed form since the first Anglo-Saxon colonization. Within are nine seats, all priced alike: three in front, three behind, three in the middle. Ladies have a right to the front seats, even if they come late. In the middle seats one is supported only by a leather strap which runs across the coach from one side to the other and takes one in the middle of the back—not exactly comfortable.

Little baggage is carried, the least possible, sometimes none at all. Shirts are of flannel and worn a long time. The collar, and if need be, the cuffs, are of paper, and are changed from time to time. The handkerchief and another article of clothing—need I be specific?—the socks, are almost unknown to the American pioneer. Why burden oneself, then, with a trunk? Besides, there is no room for bundles except the back of the coach, where there is a platform with a handrail, over which an oilcloth is fastened down.

On top of the coach we carried only the well-armed soldiers, on the watch, which is worth more than baggage. The coach is drawn by six horses, driven four-in-hand at full gallop across the prairie, level as a petrified sea. Travelers who fancy the landscape may climb up beside the driver.

From place to place, on the average every ten miles, the horses are changed. Most of the stations, veritable blockhouses, are fortified by earthen constructions of "adobe," bricks cooked in the sun. Here and there are the loophole openings. Inside the stations are also entrenchments, for a last desperate defense in case of an initial defeat. Indians sometimes arrive in numbers to surprise the isolated pioneers.

All along the route are written the ineffaceable proofs of the battle of white against the Redskin. Everywhere posthouses and farms are burned. Between the years 1864 and 1866, the stagecoach several times ceased to run. Stations were pillaged, devastated, burned; men were murdered, scalped; women and children carried into slavery. The whites took cruel revenge. Once on the Sand Creek stream in the south of Colorado, Colonel Chivington of the volunteers surprised a village of Cheyennes and Arapahos. He gave his men the order to charge,

27

despite the white flag raised by the Indians. "Remember your wives and children massacred on the Platte and the Arkansas," he said to his soldiers. The volunteers charged without pity, giving quarter to neither age nor sex. Women were disemboweled, children's heads broken against the stones, fingers and ears cut off those who wore jewelry, all heads scalped, and other horrors committed which the pen refuses to describe. More than a hundred Indians perished. The Colonel, drunk with victory, boasted everywhere of this great feat of arms, hoping to receive the stars and epaulettes of a general.

After strict and minute inquiry, the government of the Union judged him in the wrong and cashiered him; but the pioneers all declared in his favor. "A few more actions like this one," a Colorado journal wrote, "one a year, and we shall be forever delivered from these miserable Redskins who hold up our settlement." [2]

Chivington's massacre (the name generally given to the engagement at Sand Creek) was several times the subject of our conversation in the coach which took us across the prairies. Mr. Whitney, a long-time resident of Colorado, acquainted us with the details of the lamentable affair. Others of our traveling companions—the inspector of the transcontinental stage lines; an employee of the great banking house of Wells and Fargo, to which this vast enterprise belongs; an agent of the federal post office—told us further tales of the Indians. Now or never was the time to talk of the Redskins; we were, indeed, in too good and too numerous a company for them to dream of halting us.

One day, as our coach was crossing these solitudes, a naked man, perched on a rise of land, made signs to the driver. He, thinking he was

---

[2] The Sand Creek massacre of 1864 was a much disputed incident. Depredations by Sioux, Cheyennes, and Arapahos had increased in number and ferocity during the preceding two years, and travel in the Platte Valley had virtually ceased. Because the Civil War had drawn regular troops from the West, the military was unable to offer strong resistance. Colonel H. M. Chivington of the Colorado militia, prodded by criticism and bent on retaliation, attacked a band of peaceable and defenseless Cheyennes who had gathered at Sand Creek, near Fort Lyon, at the invitation of the commandant of the fort. Prospects for peace with the Indians were destroyed by this vicious and unjustified attack. Chivington's action aroused much protest, especially in the East, although western sentiment was generally in his favor. For a full account of the Chivington massacre, see Stan Hoig, *The Sand Creek Massacre* (Norman: University of Oklahoma Press, 1961).

dealing with an Indian, whipped up his horses. One of the travelers observed that he could well be a white. We paused for a moment, and the man came running and out of breath. He had just been captured by the Indians, who had stripped him of his clothing and given it to their women, or "squaws." With their customary cruelty toward the palefaces, they prepared to submit their prisoner slowly, coldly, to all the tortures which they could imagine. They would pluck out his eyes, his nails, his tongue; they would cut off a foot or a hand; they would peel off a bit of his flesh; they would tear off his skin; and finally, as a climax, they would bind the prisoner on the ground and light a fire on his abdomen, dancing an infernal circle around him. Our poor captive was about to undergo one by one all of this kind of torture when he managed to escape. The coach was passing at this moment and rescued him at the opportune time.

How many tales I could tell you of this sort! It was near one of the stations we passed through that only three years ago some poor women were surprised on a farm and taken prisoners by the Cheyennes. One of them hanged herself in despair, to escape from the expected violence. The other, forced to satisfy the passions of the chief who claimed her, was condemned to the most menial services, mistreated besides and beaten by the wives of the chief. She was separated from her children, except for one she was still nursing, and reduced almost to starvation. Sold by her master, she passed from the hands of the Cheyenne to those of a Sioux, and from him to the hands of another chief. Finally her first master came one day to buy her back to burn her alive with the young infant still at her breast. Fortunately, the sale was not concluded, and after a year of such nameless miseries the poor woman was exchanged by her tormenters for some Indian prisoners who had been seized by the whites. The mother was finally free again, but her poor children were dead. The little ones had not been able to endure the bad treatment of the Indians.

Would you not suppose you were hearing a romance or reading a page of Cooper or Irving? Well, all this happened yesterday, and if you ask in Denver or Julesburg for the name of this unhappy captive whose sufferings I have recounted, anyone will give it to you.

As our coach moved rapidly over the flat and dusty route amid the prairies, and as we passed new stations, all these stories which were told me fixed themselves in my memory. It was not for myself that I felt fear, but for the women, the young children, at each relay station. Beside the station house the ruins of buildings, the blackened timbers, gave witness to recent pillaging and burning. The Redskin is not far away; we are on his territory. He may return at any moment. Besides, is he not in open war with the whites? Nevertheless, the pioneer is always on the spot, often returning to the very same place to rebuild his ruined home. What fatal force, what mysterious law, pushes this man always forward, despite all obstacles? Pioneers of the Far West, you are the vanguard of civilization, marching with the sun; glory to you! You are neither refined nor literate, but you are useful men, virile, brave workers, energetic colonists. Savagery disappears before you, the desert is transformed before you. Obscure soldiers of progress, you will leave no name in history, though you have done great deeds; nevertheless, you push always forward, obeying the destiny which urges you on. Glory to you!

Pardon this dithyramb, my dear friend. Perhaps it is out of place in a letter; but how not admire these men of the Great West? Do you know a tale I was just told? At one of these Overland stage relay stations lost in the solitudes, Indians appeared one day, imperiously demanding food. The manager of the station was alone. He gave his unexpected visitors the best he had. The meal being finished, one of the savages said, "Now light the fire."

"For what?"

"We want to roast you. Go on. Hurry up."

The man went to his cellar on the pretext of seeking wood. The Indians followed him. He fired his revolver at one of them, mortally wounding him. The others, startled, hesitated. The man fled and hid himself in the vicinity of his house in the bushes. It was night, wintertime; the snow was falling. The Indians searched but found nothing. The fugitive dared not leave his hiding place; the snow would betray his footsteps. Finally the Indians, tired of finding nothing, left. The man returned to his station and continued to serve at his post.

In the midst of these daily anxieties the women give proof of as much coolness as the men, and as skillfully handle the rifle and revolver.

The Transcontinental Stage

At each relay station we found these arms on the table, in the corners of rooms. Have I not reason to tell you that these pioneers are men of bold hearts, and do you not now understand my dithyramb?

I must not speak more of our soldiers, whom we left one by one at the forts scattered along our route as we drew farther from the points of greatest danger. We have crossed the great American desert. Little by little the prairie has given way to fields of sand where the red ants have heaped up enormous piles of siliceous gravel, their own pyramids of Egypt. Here and there the prairie reappeared; some flowers whose brilliance was now faded still shone amid the yellowed grasses.

The weather was warm, the sky was exceedingly limpid, and for a moment we enjoyed the spectacle of a mirage. This phenomenon, in the midst of these solitudes, completed the resemblance which arose at more than one spot to the vast plains of Africa.

We encountered no hostile Indians, need I tell you, since I am writing from Denver with all my hair. I really had no luck, but what to do? Fate has so wished it. Stirring adventures will be for another time. "Driver! Driver! Stop! Look, Indians!" Someone handed the driver a telescope. It was mule drivers chasing their animals, which had taken it into their heads to quit the camp for the night. Mule drivers and drovers are our friends, traveling in long caravans on the way and sleeping at night under the stars, around their covered wagons. The stage driver went on his way without fear.

I shall tell you in my next letter of the birth of Colorado, only yesterday an unknown territory, today populous and prosperous; and that will be worth more than a recitation of Indian attacks and of scalps torn off by the brigands of the prairies. I cannot tell you lies. Black Kettle, White Antelope, Man That Walks Under the Ground, refused, like Pipelet to Cabrion, to give me their hair and had no wish to take mine.[3] Too bad!

[3] Black Kettle was the chief of the Cheyenne village that was destroyed by Chivington on Sand Creek. White Antelope, an old Cheyenne man, was killed in the Chivington massacre. Man That Walks Under the Ground, an Oglala Sioux, had been at the delegation meeting with the United States peace commission at North Platte about September 21, 1867.

Pipelet and Cabrion are characters in Eugene Sue's once popular *Mysteries of Paris*.

CHAPTER 5

The City of the Plains

Denver, Colorado, 6 October

Enough of writing about Indians; they have sown nothing but devastation and ruin. Let us speak of the whites, the palefaces, who had produced, who have created. As if by magic, they have transformed the American desert; colonized by them, the country of wild grass has changed into one of fertile fields. Climbing the Rocky Mountains to search out the veins of ore, they have planted their tents even on the farthest habitable heights and brought civilization to altitudes never before attained. You know amid what daily struggles these remarkable results have been achieved.

Denver, the true capital of Colorado, has existed but eight years.[1] It has today nearly 8,000 inhabitants; it would be double that except for the War of Secession and the war with the Indians, both of which so suddenly arrested the march of settlers toward this distant land.

The city is well built; the houses are attractive, constructed of brick, stone, or wood. Denver has numerous public buildings, a theatre, a mint, a race track. In the United States there are, properly speaking, no little cities, and Denver has a college, schools, and several newspapers, not to mention the churches, whose number already exceeds the half dozen.[2]

[1] Denver was founded in the autumn of 1858, after the discovery of gold on Cherry Creek. The rush followed in 1859.

[2] Denver's first college was the Colorado Seminary, opened in 1864. The *Rocky Mountain News* began publication in 1859, and the *Daily Rocky Mountain Herald* in 1860.

The City of the Plains

M. Tallyrand was right when he said that in North America he found but one dish and thirty-two religions. There are no cooks in this country, but everyone is a little religious.

Denver has wide streets, quite open, watered, planted with trees. It is situated on the Platte River, south branch, on either side along the stream, over which have been thrown wooden bridges, the kind the Americans know so well how to construct. Everywhere are stores, banks, hotels, saloons. As all over the Union, it is the custom to partake freely, several times a day, of the sacramental glass of whiskey, or of some of those mixed iced drinks which the 1867 Exposition revealed to the Parisians. In turn, a Frenchman has built a cafe and restaurant here, and at the foot of the Rocky Mountains worthily represents the cuisine of our country.[3] He has also all the wines of France, and the Americans are well acquainted with the path to his place.

The movement of life is everywhere. One would hardly believe himself at the end of the prairies, 2,000 miles from New York. Rapid carriages pass and repass everywhere, or heavy wagons laden with the commodities of the East, ready to leave for the mining towns. From them come only ingots of gold and silver, precious merchandise, though not as bulky. From the mountains and prairies come skins and furs, a considerable commerce in Denver.

From the agricultural areas come products which demand more space, though they are no less useful. Already the country is self-sufficient for wheat, flour, potatoes of the first quality. Garden products are also of the finest and of formidable dimensions. Only California has supplied specimens equal to those of Colorado. True, the land here is virgin and asks only to produce.

If I did not fear that you would oblige me to find the kettle to cook it in, I should tell you that I saw in Denver a cabbage which weighed more than forty-five pounds. And what a cabbage! A cabbage with a firm heart, tender, crisp leaves, green turning to white; a round cabbage, plump, majestic in form with an odor fitting its complexion.

[3] Frederick J. Charpiot, who had come to Denver in 1859, built the Charpiot Hotel in 1864, after his first restaurant was swept away by the Cherry Creek flood in the same year. His restaurant, advertised in Denver papers from 1862 on, was located on Lawrence Street, between Fifteenth and Sixteenth streets, and was for years known as the "Delmonico's of the West."

When one thinks that in these privileged climates there are such fine vegetables, and that in Paris we are served watery foods, fibrous, tasteless, one is truly tempted to import our provisions from Colorado. A day will come, doubt it not, when subterranean tubes will encircle the globe, by which, with a stroke of the piston, or at least by some pneumatic machine, we shall suck in our household supplies from one end of the earth to the other.[4] Then each country will produce only what it can, and we shall see the last of the Parisian marketplace. I would not belittle that honorable corporation, but I do say that the vegetables of Colorado and California, which I have also tasted, surpass those of the Seine basin, at the latitude of Paris. That is all.

Now I shall prudently return to Denver, to avoid trouble with anyone. Denver did not exist in 1859.[5] At that time, gold-seekers in search of placer mines at the foot of the Rocky Mountains somewhere between Santa Fe in New Mexico and Fort Laramie in Dakota, as one might say between Lisbon and Berlin, stopped on the South Platte. They washed the sands of Cherry Creek, a tributary of that river, and to their great astonishment found nuggets of gold. One is always astonished to find gold for the first time, even when one is looking for it.

The news of this happy discovery spread very quickly. Pioneers, settlers of the last states of the West, for the most part dissatisfied with their lot or thinking themselves so, came hurrying with the crowd of "squatters," desperate men, all the adventurers so numerous in the states watered by the Mississippi and the Missouri. As elsewhere, there was disorder without a name; but the law of lynch and the vigilance committees soon dealt out justice to all thieves and assassins, and order was almost immediately restored.

I have heard about these troubled beginnings. Before the city was yet in existence, emigrants were arriving in caravans and camping in their wagons for lack of other shelter. It required several weeks to travel from the Mississippi to the foot of the Rocky Mountains. No stagecoach, no railroad yet came that way. Redskins all too often lay in wait on the way, and one had to come to terms with them, pay for the right of passage over their territory, or, if need be, dispute for one's

[4] Pneumatic tubes for the carrying of mail had been the subject of experiments in London and Paris, as well as in Germany, during the 1850's.
[5] Simonin is in error here. See footnote 1, above.

life. However, they were not quite as savage as they were to become, when the settlement of Colorado began to take parts of their lands from them, and when the War of Secession gave them hope and united them against a common and divided foe.

Despite all these obstacles, the emigrants arrived in crowds. New placer mines were discovered every day. Added to them were mines bearing gold in veins, quartz mines, as they were called, because the quartz, or crystal, of the compact rock in which the gold floats forms the principal material. Fortunes were founded from one day to the next, and sometimes were lost with the same ease in gaming or dissipation. But winners only, never losers, are remembered; and Colorado had its fever, its "excitement," as California, with its inexhaustible deposits, had had; as had Lake Superior, with its copper mines, Nevada, with its silver veins, and Petrolia, with its wells of oil and gasoline.[6] In such matters of colonizing, the United States proceeds as by a mine fever, and right now all await some new event, for no excitement of this sort has taken place now for several years.[7]

The excitement in Colorado reached its peak from the first days, and the bankers of New York, Boston, and Philadelphia vied with one another in lending their money for these hazardous enterprises, when they could not come themselves to manage affairs on the spot. At first, there had been a moment of doubt, of hesitation. The "Pikes-pikers" [sic], or miners on Pikes Peak (so called as a play on words, Pike, peak, pick, because the first discovery of gold had taken place, so to speak, at the foot of the peak by that name, one of the few points known at that time in the Rocky Mountains),—the Pikes Peakers were at first regarded as dreamers, if not worse. I was then in California (1859), and I recall that the discovery of gold on the plains of the Far West was treated as a "humbug." In their turn, the newspapers of the western states argued that the samplings of the Pikes Peakers were nothing but California nuggets. Finally, however, they had their eyes opened, and the excitement was the greater because of the moment of reaction. Everybody came running, everyone wanted his share of the plunder.

[6] Petrolia, Ontario, became the first "oil capital" of Canada in 1861.

[7] The discovery of gold on the Sweetwater, territory of Wyoming, in the Rocky Mountains, and especially of silver mines at White Pine, state of Nevada, came successively during 1868, and justified these prognostications. [*Simonin's note.*]

35

I cannot reflect on such events without recalling that it was for similar reasons that all heads in France were turned at the time of Law's bank. The Scotch economist, whom history has not yet judged as he deserves, was the more inspired in his projects for colonizing the plains of the Mississippi because these plains were then claimed by us, and because the country where gold and silver has been so recently discovered, Colorado, unknown yesterday and destined to be so powerful tomorrow, is precisely situated in that Mississippi basin which Law wished to make fruitful. The great man arose too soon. His genius had suspected what really existed: the inexhaustible subterranean wealth of these magnificent lands. But the hour had not yet sounded for their exploitation, and besides, nature had reserved the labor of developing these deserts for another people than our own. Law was neither impostor nor adventurer; he was a great economist, and even more, a man sprung up before his time. He was an American type before the American was born.[8]

The territory of Colorado, settled principally by the exploitation of gold, demonstrates that Law's dreams were realities. If the emerald mines of which he spoke do not exist and have not yet been discovered along the Mississippi, it is nonetheless true that the lead mines for which he obtained the concession, those of Missouri, Illinois, and Wisconsin, constitute today part of the wealth of those states, and are the most productive in the world. It is no less true that the gold mines of Colorado, solely by their development and in less than eight years, have given rise to a happy and prosperous territory to which pioneers would not have come without the lure of the precious metal, in all times the surest agent of distant colonization.

At first there was no one in Colorado. The country had not even a name. It was part of the territory of Kansas,[9] and the name Colorado belongs to a river which descends from the opposite slope of the Rocky

[8] John Law (1671–1729) was controller-general of finances in France and organizer of the famous "Mississippi scheme," whereby the French government backed its paper money with shares in its India Company and North American possessions under government monopoly. The collapse of the "system" brought about general bankruptcy.

[9] Organized in 1861, Colorado Territory was in reality carved from parts of the territories of Kansas, Nebraska, Utah, and New Mexico.

Mountains and rushes toward the Gulf of California. The Spaniards had so named it because its banks in certain places are colored by oxidized iron-bearing soils, and the river itself is therefore red, *colorado*.

Only now and then did some rare trapper go through this country to hunt the fur-bearing animals, the bison, the beaver, the bear, or to barter with the Indians. The Utes lodged in the plateaus of these mountains, the "parks," as they are called, and were always at war with the Cheyennes and Arapahos of the prairies.

It would have taken years to settle these deserted plains. But a happy accident helped adventurers discover what scholars, explorers, geologists, even engineers, who had passed a number of times through these latitudes, had not noted, gold mines! And settlers came hastening, and the country was established. There where the bison roamed with the Redskins on his track, a village was born, and another. A new territory, then a new state will soon be added to those which already make up the Union. Tomorrow another star will shine in the tri-colored starry flag, a new star to increase the power of this land without in any sense disturbing its unity. Is not the American motto: *E pluribus unum*?

Do you know what Denver was at first christened? *Auraria*, gold mine. Since then the name has been changed to Denver in honor of the governor of Kansas.[10] Some rebels (where do you not find them?) wished for a time to call Denver the City of the Plains, because of its situation in the midst of the prairies. Despite the happy choice of this name, they did not succeed, and Denver it remains.

Since gold should not be forgotten, they named the capital of the young territory, if not the same Auraria, at least Golden City.[11] Golden City is a small town of 1,000 inhabitants, which I shall visit tomorrow and perhaps write you from there. Contrary to the European custom, capitals in America are always the least populated cities, an understandable thing in purely democratic states.

The chamber of representatives and senators is at Golden City, and

[10] Auraria, originally a rival settlement, was consolidated with Denver in 1860. Denver was named in honor of James W. Denver, governor of Kansas Territory (1858).

[11] Actually, Golden City was named for Tom Golden, an early prospector. Founded in 1859, it served as territorial capital from 1862 until late 1867, when the capital was moved to Denver.

the seat of the territorial government, though Denver is truly the commercial center for Colorado.

I must say a word of the society of this country, as it first struck me. Denver, you know, was settled as though by the wave of a fairy wand. It is said that the pioneers of this Far West went out on the prairies with a roll of twine in their pockets and a dozen stakes in their hands, and that, once arrived on a favorable spot, they planted their stakes in the earth, marked off the streets and houses with the twine, and said, "Here will be Babylon, Thebes, Memphis, etc." Fine, but Babylon, Thebes, Memphis, especially in the United States, must have people. Who were, who are the inhabitants of Denver, born scarcely eight years ago?

Rest assured. They were not here, as in other regions, a mixture of all nations, and in large part the scum of all nations. Only the pioneers of the last western states came. There were some troubles at the outset, as I have said; but it was all between Americans, and in the American manner, and calm quickly returned. The better people, being in the majority from the start, permanently dispersed the others. The pioneers arrived with their families, their wives and children, and from the first day society was formed on the eternally enduring foundations.

Comfort, the habits of domestic life, the "home," cherished alike by Americans and Englishmen, were quickly revived, re-established, by the Colorado pioneers, and today you would be amazed to meet so much refinement and well-being in the midst of these regions.

I have seen ladies here whom New York or Boston would envy or regret losing. We dined yesterday with Senator Evans, former governor of Colorado.[12] The society was select and animated, and we conversed as in a Paris salon, or, shall we say, as in the drawing room of the most cultivated Americans. Conversation turned particularly on the International Exposition at Paris, which is followed with a lively interest in all this country.

Our amiable companion, Mr. Whitney, commissioner from Colorado at the Exposition, who brought back a gold medal to his adopted territory, is everywhere acclaimed and entertained. It was in his honor

[12] John Evans (1814–1897) was appointed by President Lincoln as second territorial governor of Colorado in 1862. He served until 1865.

that Mr. Evans had gathered some of his friends at dinner. The newspapers vie with each other in celebrating the fame of the fortunate commissioner, and the talk is all of sending him as territorial representative to Washington. He is indeed the representative man of Colorado.

I already delight in this young country, so earnestly going about its business. Therefore I shall write at greater length of it in my next letter, which I shall date from Golden City.

CHAPTER 6

The Founders of Colorado

In my last letter, dated Denver, October 6, I wrote that I would say more of the territory of Colorado, and would write from its capital, Golden City. But I was unable to carry out this project at the time of my passing through the City of Gold, where I arrived rather late at night on my return from a visit to the coal mines of Boulder. Nature has given everything to this rich country.

At dawn the following day we took the stage which was to convey us to one of the highest inhabited spots in the Rocky Mountains, Central City, a city well named for us, for it has been a sort of center from which we have ranged outward in all our explorations.

On horseback from morning, for three weeks we have visited all the mines, all the alpine locations of this singular territory, sometimes scaling the highest summits, sometimes traversing the deepest valleys. Bernadines and Benedictines would have been equally happy if they had been in our party, for if the first, on the example of their master, loved the valleys, the latter did not disdain the hills: *Bernardus valles, colles Benedictus amabat.*

During all this time I have deserted the pen for the miner's hammer, and that is why you have received no letters. I have descended into the deepest pits and entered the winding galleries; I have visited the placer mines and inspected the smelters where the gold and silver ores are treated; and I have carried away from all my excursions the most

40

favorable impressions of the activity and the intelligence everywhere demonstrated by the Colorado pioneers.

We have made our journeys on horseback, riding from morning to evening, sometimes for several days in a row. I have found here the same excellent Mexican animals that I had already mounted in California, which will go for twelve hours at a trot or gallop, without stopping, without eating, content to snatch some sprigs from bushes en route, when such are along the path. They also want to drink at every stream. Let them quench their thirst, if such is their pleasure. Good beasts! And how they do justice to their stable fare in the evening! Indefatigable, they do nevertheless weary the rider, and I must admit to you that yesterday evening when I arrived at Georgetown, the central city of silver mining as Central City is that for gold mining, I let myself slide from my mount, crying the cry of the Peruvian president Castilla: *No puedo mas*, I can do no more! Thus the old president fell a few months ago, on his way to Arequipa, giving up his soul to another world.[1] I fell like him before the hotel in Georgetown, but to pick myself up again and to proceed to dine and sleep.

We have traveled on horseback like the Castilians who, even today, cannot visit most of the mines in their country in any other way. But do not think that roads are lacking here, even though we are in mountainous country. Stagecoaches, of the type you know, go everywhere; relay stations are set up everywhere, restaurants, saloons. On these roads, opened in part by nature, in part by man, and very badly maintained by the latter, on such roads, where it is rare to meet a road worker, and which are supervised by no official commission of highways and bridges, the dust rises in thick whirlwinds as the coach advances, swiftly, six horses on the gallop. One is literally powdered and blinded, especially in a country where not a drop of water falls for six months at a time. At the relay stations, a basin and a pitcher of water awaits you, with soap and a towel that turns without end around a roller. You will find mirrors, combs, brushes of all kinds, even toothbrushes, fastened by a long string, so that everyone may help himself

[1] Ramon Castilla (*ca.* 1797–1867) was president of Peru from 1845 to 1851 and again from 1858 to 1862. Arequipa, Peru's second city, was the center of revolution, 1865–1867.

and no one carry it off. You would laugh in Paris at these democratic customs; here they are accepted by all and even welcomed, unless perhaps the toothbrush, which is regarded with a suspicious eye.

How often in all the Great West, on all the roads and railroads, have I blessed this charitable water and these toilet articles so freely offered to all! Recall what one endures in summer on our French railroads, where certain of these customs should surely be made a part of our principal stations, granted generously, as an expected thing, and without obligation to pay.

If the dust is the traveler's chief enemy in this plains country, in the mountains there is the jolting of the stagecoach, of which you can form no idea. The vehicle rolls at full gallop down the dizziest heights, over great boulders and blocks of stone. Impassive at his post, the driver drives his six steeds with a sure hand. One wonders that he is never thrown from his seat; he seems to be held there by straps. Inside, the travelers suffer, bruised and racked by the jolting. Some are seasick from the rolling and pitching so new to them.

Nevertheless, this type of travel is general all over the United States. I have found it even in California. The story is told that a few years ago the famous New York journalist, Mr. Horace Greeley, expected at San Francisco for some convention or lectures, went by the Overland stage. As he was crossing the heights of the Sierra Nevadas, and the stage did not go fast enough to suit him, he feared that he might be late in arriving. Announcements were already out and the day set. So he begged the driver to whip up his horses and go a little faster.

"Hang on to your seat," the man answered; "I'll get you there on time."

And slackening the reins and urging his animals on vigorously, he started the carriage at full speed down a precipitous descent. The journalist protested, cried out, and stormed, but to no avail. "Hang on to your seat, Mr. Greeley, and you'll get there on time," the driver shouted, his eyes smiling, his mouth mocking.

Mr. Greeley did indeed arrive on the hour, and forgetting all grudge, recompensed his tormenter by making him a present of a new suit of clothes. The tale has remained legendary among travelers of the Far West, and the driver, still effectively employed, has had his reply to Mr. Greeley engraved on the case of his watch: "Hang on, Mr. Greeley, and you'll get there on time!" It is even said that the watch was given as a souvenir to this good fellow, if not by the impatient journalist, at least by some travelers who had made the trip with the same driver, and who had heard the same tale.[2]

All means of rapid locomotion, certainly, have always been regarded by Americans as one of the surest means of their vast colonization. You have seen that Colorado is no less committed to these ideas. From the days of the birth of this territory, the Overland Mail has been a part of it, changing its routes as the new country was settled, asking no aid from the federal government, and no indemnity.

Everyone moves about here with his business, and never remains fixed in the corner he has once chosen.

I have written overlong about the Overland Mail. The most striking wonder carried out by the Americans across the Great West was that of the "pony." This service was born in California in 1860, and functioned up to the day when one continuous telegraph line linked the Pacific to the Missouri, and from there to the Atlantic.[3]

In six days, by means of the rapid horse, or "pony," they spanned the distance of 1,600 miles, or 650 leagues, which then existed between the extreme limit of the telegraph in the Atlantic states and the young state on the Pacific. Horse and rider were replaced at each station, and the beast set off at a gallop, sometimes stopped en route by the Redskin, who lay in wait for the courier to kill him and steal his horse. The service was nonetheless astonishing, and by such means dispatches from Europe of October 21 reached San Francisco on November 12, 1860, that is, dated scarcely twenty days earlier, and the news of the presidential election of November 6, which gave the majority to Lincoln, the abolitionist candidate. Today the telegraph has replaced the pony, and you may receive a dispatch from Paris in San Francisco before the hour when it was sent, thanks to the speed of electricity and the difference in meridians.

[2] Horace Greeley, editor of the *New York Tribune*, in 1859 traveled by one of the first stagecoaches from Leavenworth, Kansas, to the Colorado mines and on to San Francisco. His account, *An Overland Journey* (1860), stimulated interest in the new West.

[3] The Pony Express operated from April, 1860, to March, 1862, when telegraph service between the East Coast and the West Coast was established.

The services of the stagecoach, pony, and telegraph seem thus to have been timed precisely for the settlement of Colorado, when the first pioneers arrived: all that was needed was man to complete the work for which so many material advantages had set the stage.

The pioneer! I have never seen him so virile, so great, or with such morale. We stopped in Central City at the home of one of the most respected families of the country, that of Mr. W. A. Whiting, agent for Mr. Whitney's mines.[4] The most cordial hospitality was extended to us by these fine folk, and the graceful cottage which is their home was still further beautified to receive us.

Mr. Whiting has wife and children with him. Two of his daughters are married and live under the same roof with their father, and with their families. In this busy beehive everyone has his or her task: the men go every day to their work, the young boys and girls to school, the women to their household cares. There are no domestics; they are not to be found, or they cost too much, twenty francs, or around four dollars a day!

At evening all come together: they talk, read, make music; the ladies do needlework, the children mingle their noisy play with the calmer distractions of the older folk. Such is the honest and austere family of the pioneer; each has planted his penates there for good, with no thought of turning back.

What wonderful days my companions and I spent in that hospitable home! What pleasant memories we have carried away with us! Never the slightest cloud arose in the midst of all these people, of such diverse spirit and character. And what I say of this family could apply to a hundred others whom I met at Black Hawk, Nevada, Idaho, Empire, Georgetown, and elsewhere. I am not speaking of Denver society, which I have already depicted for you.

Mr. Whiting and his family came from Illinois during the first days of the discovery of gold at the foot of the Rocky Mountains. They had a farm in that state, but sold it to try their fortunes in the Far West. All came, men, wives, children, quite aware that the only serious

[4] In 1867 W. A. Whiting was director of the Bullion Consolidated Mining Company in Central City, and "Agent in Colorado" for J. P. Whitney, its treasurer, until November.

44

pioneers and settlers are those who bring with them all their household possessions, their penates, like Aeneas saying farewell to Ilium.

In these distant mines, in these uncultivated valleys, I have found others of these brave emigrants. The cottage is in the midst of the forest, lost in rugged mountain scenery, or in the shadowy valley. You enter: a gracious woman receives you; the husband earnestly offers you shelter under his roof and a share in his meal. The linen is gleaming white; the most varied dishes adorn the table, often prepared by delicate hands but lately accustomed to other occupations. Everywhere are fine furniture, habits of luxury, comfort, such as one is astonished to find in these distant deserts.

Naturally, the picture is not everywhere the same. I should like now to describe some new types of pioneers, whom I shall call adventurers, rovers, the lost children of colonization. Married or bachelors, they form a band apart. I should like also to say a word of the gold and silver mines. You frown. Have no fear. I shall not go too much into geology. Besides, I shall reserve all this for another letter. One should not treat of two subjects at the same time: *non bis idem*, as the Latin says—spoken even in these mountains.

CHAPTER 7

The Miners of the Rocky Mountains

Central City, in the Rocky Mountains, 25 October

Here we are, once again with our amiable hosts of whom I wrote in my preceding letter. Elsewhere we have camped only; here we have dwelt for a time.

Everyone has received us with an eager friendliness. You recall our reception in Denver; at Georgetown, the very city itself asked to entertain us. When we asked the hotelkeeper for our bill, we were told that the municipal council expected to take care of it. In Central City the band welcomed us, from the first evening of our arrival, with the sound of its brass instruments, playing its whole repertoire, and further, no doubt to pay honor to the Frenchman who was there, the Marseillaise. True, this last was so subdued that if it had been played in the same way to our volunteers of '93, they assuredly would not have marched to battle in such high spirits. But perhaps it was the effect of the climate. Music, like ideas, may change with the latitude, and what is the Marseillaise on the 49th parallel in Europe may turn into a pastorale on the 40th in America.

Everywhere, to please the public, we had to give talks—lectures, they are called in the United States, because the speaker has the habit of reading.[1] Listeners came in numbers to hear us, eager to learn. Here an organization placed its hall at our disposal; there a clergyman graciously lent his church when the halls of the Mechanics' Institute were not large enough to accommodate the crowd.

[1] *Lecture* in French means a reading.

46

The Miners of the Rocky Mountains

Colonel Heine spoke on the Pacific railroad, Mr. Whitney on our Paris Exposition, and I, before all these miners, touched on the question so alive to them, gold and silver.[2]

I like these vigorous, proud men who seek their well-being only in themselves and count on no other to accomplish for them. In Colorado, as in all the Union, they practice the great Anglo-Saxon maxim: Help yourself!

I have already written of the pioneers who have come here with their families. There is protection, a better defense, in numbers; but many emigrants have come entirely alone and have not lost courage even so. I met several of these intrepid hermits the other day among the mines of Trail Creek, in a narrow valley hidden in the midst of pine trees and surrounded by snow-clad peaks. One of them, a Dr. Howland from Boston (why should I not name him?), surprised me by his stoic calm.[3] Though from an excellent family and provided with the best education, he had left the surgeon's scalpel for the miner's pick. One of the first, he left for the placer mines of Colorado, and today controls a gold-bearing quartz mine and a mechanical mill for crushing and amalgamating the rock.

The first time I met the doctor he showed me with a certain pride the beautiful nuggets he himself had found. On a plank fastened to the wall of his cabin were some books of applied science, treatises on chemistry, metallurgy, the operation of mines, a course in mineralogy. Some of these books were written in French. There was also a souvenir of his first studies, a Galen in the original Latin.

"I amuse myself by reading," the doctor said.

And when I asked him if this exile in the depths of the forest and in so somber a valley was not distressing to him, he answered, "I don't care for society. I am well off here, and here I stay."

[2] See Appendix, p. 162.

[3] Trail Creek is a small valley west of Idaho Springs, on the way to Georgetown and Empire.

There is no record of a Dr. Howland in the area at that time, although "Captain Jack" Howland accompanied Simonin's party to Fort Laramie as an artist (see below, p. 78). However, a Dr. Henry H. Hewitt went to California Gulch and Oro City (which Simonin calls Oroville) in 1863 and there divided his time between mining and medicine. In 1866 he moved from Oro City to the Georgetown area. (Oro City was destined to boom again in 1878 as Leadville.) It would appear that Hewitt is the doctor to whom Simonin refers.

47

"But does not the Bible say: Woe to him who lives alone! *Vae soli?*"

"The Bible does not say that to me."

The place where the doctor formerly lived, now deserted, was once livelier and more animated. A row of cabins in ruins, for the most part built of logs and mud, true "log-houses" of the poor pioneers, once answered to the sonorous name of Oroville. The placer mines were soon exhausted, and with them faded the hopes of the seekers, who left, undaunted, to expend their efforts elsewhere. They could not, like Bias,[4] take their houses with them on their shoulders. Oroville, scarcely born, is already a city in ruins.

Some few exceptional miners, tenacious, indefatigable, stubborn prospectors, remained with Dr. Howland. Ranging over the mountains as the valley failed them, they soon uncovered on the tributary flanks of Trail Creek some veins of gold-bearing quartz. Thanks to the liberal laws governing the operation of mines in all the Union, they were able, aside from some elementary formalities, to lay claim on the spot to full and entire ownership of the site for a certain length of time and an indefinite depth.

One of these prospectors is the Frenchman Chavanne, whom I have twice encountered in these regions, always at work, sturdy, enterprising, and giving for his part a very good impression of workers from our country. But Chavanne is not satisfied; he wants to see his native land again, the province of Franche-Comte.

"Ah, Mr. engineer," he said to me a few days ago, "if you could set up a company for me in Paris to develop these veins, I would give them to you for nothing and return to France to see my old father. I very much want to return to the homeland."

"But, Chavanne, there or here, one has always to work."

"True, sir; but America, you see, is not France."

"Why don't you do like these Americans here who come with no hope of turning back and settle even to the highest plateaus of the Rocky Mountains?"

"The Americans are at home; I haven't had any luck. I earned money in New York at plating glass; but mercury is a wicked metal, and besides, that was what gave me the idea of working in the gold mines.

[4] Bias, one of the Seven Wise Men of Greece, in flight took nothing with him, as a sign that his most valued possessions were in his mind.

The Miners of the Rocky Mountains

At first I earned a lot. Now things are not going so well, and I'd like to dispose of the mines I have left. If you could set up a company in Paris, I'd give them to you for nothing."

While talking, Chavanne did me the honors of his log house. He showed me the map, nailed to the wall, of the gold-bearing district of Trail Creek, covered with a network of veins, real or imaginary, found in the area by the seekers, or prospectors, as they are called.

These hunters of metallic veins, these *coureurs* of the mountains, who recall the *buscones* or *cateadores* of Peru and Chile, the *gambusinos* and *rebuscadores* of Mexico, have produced from the first some illustrious examples in Colorado.[5] It was one of them, Gregory, a former miner in the gold-bearing state of Georgia, who discovered the famous vein at Central City which bears his name. This was at the beginning of the development.[6] "If the streams at the foot of the Rocky Mountains carry gold," said Gregory, "the mountains must contain it." So he set out alone, on foot, clambering up the steep slopes of valleys which none had ever entered before. He carried his provisions and tools on his back. After several days he came to the spot where Central City now lies, at more than 2,500 metres [over 8,000 feet] in elevation, and there found the vein he sought, and gold nuggets as large as nuts.

But Gregory was out of provisions and a snowstorm was brooding. Was he to perish, like some conquerors, in the midst of his triumph? He descended to Auraria, city of the plains, now Denver, and there took a friend into his confidence on his discovery. The two returned to the site, worked it with energy, and after a few days returned to the city laden with gold. The noise of this discovery very soon spread abroad, and an army of miners penetrated to the valleys of the Rocky Mountains.

[5] These Spanish-American terms mean, respectively, seekers; wielders of the *cateador*, or prospector's hammer; again seekers or prospectors; and placer miners. *Gambusinos* is from Californian *gamble-business*, according to the *Diccinario General de Americanismos* (Mexico City, 1942).

[6] In 1858 John Gregory, a miner and former Georgian, found evidence of gold on Clear Creek. Keeping his secret, he returned the following spring and in May discovered the first important lode of gold-bearing quartz in Colorado, near the site of Central City, thus precipitating the rush. Within a matter of months, Gregory Gulch, comprising the towns of Central City, Black Hawk, Nevadaville, Georgetown, Empire, and Idaho Springs, was organized as a district. See Donald C. Kemp, *Colorado's Little Kingdom* (Golden, Colo.: Sage Books, 1949).

Such was the origin of the metal-bearing development at Central City; such are the facts which gave birth to this city and the neighboring ones of Black Hawk and Nevada.

The discovery of the silver mines of Georgetown arose from similar circumstances. One fine day in 1864, "Governor" Steele[7]—whom I had the pleasure of meeting in Georgetown, and who received his title, I believe, because he had some hope of being nominated for governor of Colorado—set out with some friends.

"Let's climb to the top of the mountains," he said to his friends; "there must be some silver mines up there." So one group went up one side, the others by another. They met on the Snake Range at an elevation of nearly 3,500 metres, nearly 11,500 feet; and they remained for several days on the peaks and in the valleys. Finally one of the prospectors uncovered a very rich vein of silver ore.[8]

It is by such men and by such means that Colorado was framed and developed, and by whom the working of the mines has more and more advanced. At Georgetown, aside from the Governors Steele, Patterson, and others, I met more nomadic prospectors, true adventurers of the mountains—for example, the American Brown, who has discovered his share of the veins.[9]

"I climb to the highest ridges," he told me, "entirely alone, carrying my own pick and hammer and provisions for several days. I search, I smell out, I scratch the soil; and little by little, under the grass, I end by finding the heads of metallic veins. I recognize them by the lines of whitish quartz, decomposed, rotted, yellowed by iron, sometimes stained with shining points of steel-gray. Finally I uncover the veins and that is what I want. Then, alone, I take the compass and rod, I claim the site, that is to say, I define my property geometrically. As the finder, I have the right, you know, to 5,000 feet of vein. I have my claim

[7] Robert W. Steele, an Iowa lawyer, was elected first governor of Jefferson Territory, an illegal government established without Congressional sanction in 1859 and replaced in 1861, with the admission of Colorado Territory to the Union.

[8] Steele was reputed to have been one of the first to discover silver in the Georgetown area, in 1864.

[9] E. N. H. Patterson was editor of the Georgetown *Colorado Miner*. The Brown referred to here was probably Frank Brown, who struck it rich in the Gregory Gulch diggings in the spring of 1862.

recorded with the recorder or clerk of the district. I pay the charge, not much—four dollars, twenty francs in your money—and that's that. My vein is carried on the register of the district under the name I have given it. I am the sole proprietor. I have some for sale. Are you interested?"

And Brown showed me lines of veins on the high summits of Georgetown, running out of sight to the very foot of the glaciers, and which it would take a whole day to reach by climbing.

This prospector was clad in a costume of deerskin, with fringes, and adorned with embroidery in arabesque designs. He had leather breeches like those of the Redskins, and wore the pioneer's big boots and the broad-brimmed felt hat of the prairie trapper.

"All this cost me $200," he told me; "I have for a long time wanted to go to Paris. I want to walk up and down the boulevard in my trapper costume. Do you think I'd cut a figure?"

"You should have gone to Paris this year, Brown. You would have been a public curiosity at the Exposition on the Champ de Mars, along with the Japanese and the little Chinese on exhibit there, alongside the industrial products."

"It's too late now, but you will see me someday on the boulevards in my costume, you may be sure."

What do you think of these energetic workers, my friend, you who read this letter at ease in Paris? Do you agree that they worthily represent the vanguard of civilization in the Great West? Is it not so? And they represent it without distinction of nationality. If I had time and did not fear to tire your attention, I should pass before you further types of miners and pioneers: the Spaniard Dominguez, married to a Frenchwoman; the mine captains from English Cornwall; the prospectors, the exploiters of lodes, Irish, Germans, Italians, Canadians, French. In short, you would review an honest and virile legion of workers, each with the distinctive characteristics of his race, and all with the common trait of persistence, energy, coolness, good pioneers and true colonists. But enough for today; I shall write soon of the mines, having now described the miners.

CHAPTER 8

Gold and Silver

Golden City, at the foot of the Rocky Mountains, 26 October

At the moment of saying farewell to Colorado, where I have passed such well-filled days, I shall write further of its mines of gold and silver. I might add a discourse on coal, found everywhere at a small distance below the prairie sod; or iron, which lies alongside the coal; or salt, which is found in abundance in the "parks" (the name given to the high wooded and grassy plateaus where the Utes live); or the sulphur waters, alkaline, effervescent, which gush from the earth in so many places. But gold and silver outrank all other exploitation here, as is but just. Did they not give birth to the country, did they not make possible its peopling, its development? Here, as in the forming of all society, the working of metallic mines preceded everything else, even agriculture; here, as everywhere, the pick preceded the plow.

From the first days, as I have already written, everyone has abandoned himself to the lodes with unexampled zeal. A veritable fever has existed for the extraction of these subterranean riches; and all the bankers of the eastern states have competed in lending their capital, sending their agents into the territory, where they thought for a moment to see a second California born.

The reaction came swiftly, not only because of the War of Secession and the Indian wars, both of which turned the flood of emigrants from this young colony, but for other reasons as well, perhaps no less serious, which I must now dwell upon and ask your full attention.

52

Gold and Silver

In the placer mines, properly so called, gold is found in particles, in nuggets, and the metal is always in its native state, or pure metal. Because of its great weight, there is no difficulty in separating it from the sands amid which it is found; a more or less improved method of washing suffices, done with rather ingenious apparatus. The lighter matter runs off with the water, the gold remains. Amalgamation may also be employed, that is, attacking the gold with mercury. Mercury, as you know, has the property of dissolving gold, precisely as water dissolves sugar, and of returning it by distillation so neatly that you might say in popular terms in this case that gold is like the candied sugar of mercury.

But it is a quite different matter with the lode ores. Here, that is, in Colorado, the gold is no longer in its native state, but in a *sulfurate* state, as they say in America, or, if you prefer, in a state of close combination with sulphurs, iron, lead, copper, zinc, from which it is very difficult to extract it in its entirety.

Silver very often accompanies gold. Alone or allied to gold, silver is never pure, but always in a sulfurate state, whether simple or multiple, or in combination with chloride, iodide, bromide, etc. All these combinations are usually quite complex, and it is almost as difficult as with gold to extract all the silver contained in these ores.

I do not wish here to give you a dissertation on metallurgy, no more than I tired you with geology on the subject of the location of these mines. I wish only to explain that by the most delicate processes of pulverization; by calcination (oxidizing by heat), or passing through fire, with or without steam; by amalgamation, or dissolution in mercury; by chloridization, or attack by marine salt, chloride, chlorohydric acid, which decomposes the metallic sulphurs, by all these processes, one never succeeds in recovering more than three-fourths of the gold and silver in compound in these Colorado ores. Often even only a third or a half, sometimes scarcely a fourth of these precious metals is "saved," as the miners say.

This fact had already come to notice in California, where they have still to discover a definitive process for metallurgic treatment; but nowhere as in Colorado have all the mines at once had to wrestle with the same difficulty, apparently an almost insurmountable one.

Here the problem to be resolved is more than ever critical; on its solution actually depends in part the future of the territory. Even though everyone, from the first day, has applied himself to the task, chemists, metallurgists, engineers, scholars (I do not include captains of industry or counterfeiters), and though each, in a kind of steeplechase, has brought forward the process he thinks best, no process has as yet succeeded, and the prize awaits the fortunate inventor of a treatment for the natural gold-silver-bearing sulphurs. He who finds the means of reducing, *by practical methods*, not those of the laboratory, the ores of Colorado, and collaterally those of Montana, Idaho, Nevada, and California, all harassed by the same problem, all this quantity of gold and silver which they contain, revealed by analysis, he will have made his fortune. Overnight he would be rich in the millions, and, at the same time, would have given the most fruitful impetus to the settlement of the states and territories of the Great West. It would be a fortune well earned. He would be a true inventor, and not one of those who painfully seek the counterfeiting of processes already known.

But what am I saying—the true inventor? He who will bring to Colorado the method of metallurgic treatment so long awaited would be not only the benefactor of the territory and of all the Far West; he should also be solemnly proclaimed one of the benefactors of the human race, so fertile would the invention be in results. To the task, metallurgists! Which of you will become the great man whom the world awaits?

And you, who receive these letters in Paris, call on the French masters of chemistry, and they are many, to light their furnaces for this great research, and to show themselves once more, as they have done in so many other circumstances, the worthy successors of Lavoisier, Berthollet, Thénard.[1]

North America's is a singular destiny, that of being not only the country of the future, toward which gravitate all of today's emigrants, all colonists, the country which in a short time may perhaps change the laws of the political and commercial world, but of being also the country

---

[1] Antoine Laurent Lavoisier (1743–1794), Claude Louis Berthollet (1748–1822), and Louis Jacques Thénard (1777–1857) all made major contributions to modern chemistry.

which at this moment produces most of the gold and silver of the whole globe.

From one ocean to the other, whether one follows the littoral chain of the Atlantic, the Appalachian Mountains, the Alleghenies, or whether one crosses the central chain of the great continent, the Rocky Mountains, from which I write you at this moment, or the chain which looks upon the Pacific, the Sierra Nevadas, everywhere are scattered the placer mines, the lodes of gold and silver; everywhere, at the foot, on the flanks, at the summit of these mountains, run the subterranean veins of these metals. Just when one thinks the veins exhausted, new mines appear. After the gold locations of California, the richest and most extensive of which history makes mention, silver-bearing mines are discovered in Nevada, alone richer than all those of Spanish America. Then came the gold and silver mines of Colorado, Idaho, Montana, Oregon, Arizona, some of which challenge the preceding for wealth and extent of veins, for abundance of production.

This is a new fact in the history of North America, to furnish today more than half of the billion francs in gold and silver produced annually by the whole globe.[2] This fact has been only recently observed, but it has not escaped the notice of the men who govern the Union. Every year the President, in his message, makes known the statistical details of the production of gold and silver, and from year to year generally finds occasion to congratulate the country on the results and the progress achieved.

One is not content just to know in the United States; one must see. Thus the mines of the Great West, so talked about in the world, are the

[2] Here, according to official information, is what must have been the production of gold and silver in the United States in 1867, one of the most favorable years.

California	125,000,000 fr.
Nevada	100,000,000
Montana	60,000,000
Idaho	30,000,000
Colorado	25,000,000
Oregon	10,000,000
Other states and territories	25,000,000
Total production of gold and silver in the U.S., 1867	375,000,000 fr.

[*Simonin's note.*]

The sums are given in francs; approximately five francs equal one dollar.

object of many visits, not only by scientists and engineers, but as well by journalists, and statesmen of the Union. One of the best-known political figures in America, and one of the most moderate, Mr. Colfax, who seems likely to be named Vice-President by public voice in the next elections if General Grant is chosen President, has recounted in one of his many "speeches" his visit in 1865 to the gold and silver mines of the Far West. He was at that time president, "speaker," of the House of Representatives in Washington, and took advantage of one of the interim periods when the House was not in session to see, as he said, the real miners, the real Indians, the real Mormons of the Far West. He set out by the Overland Mail, accompanied by a few friends, among others a journalist from Springfield, Massachusetts, a Mr. Bowles, who has left an interesting description of this trip.[3] On the eve of his departure, the 14th of April, Mr. Colfax went to take leave of the President.

"I want you," said Mr. Lincoln, "to take a message from me to the miners whom you visit. I have very large ideas of the mineral wealth of our nation. I believe it to be practically inexhaustible. It abounds all over the western country, from the Rocky Mountains to the Pacific, and the development has scarcely commenced. During the war, when we were adding a couple millions every day to our national debt, I did not care about encouraging the increase in the volume of our precious metals. We had the country to save first, but now that the rebellion is overthrown and we know pretty nearly the amount of our national debt, the more gold and silver we mine, we make the payment of that debt so much the easier.

"Now," he said, speaking with more emphasis, "I am going to encourage that in every possible way. We shall have hundreds of thousands of disbanded soldiers, and many have feared that the return home in

[3] Schuyler Colfax (1823–1885) was a representative to Congress from Indiana (1855–1869) and Speaker of the House of Representatives from 1863 to 1869. He later served as Vice-President under Grant (1869–1873). His visit to Central City and speech there are recorded in the Central City *Daily Miners' Register* for June 1, 1865.

With Samuel Bowles (1826–1878), a prominent journalist and publisher of the Springfield, Massachusetts, *Daily Republican*, he traveled to California by Overland stage in 1865. Bowles subsequently published *Across the Continent* (1865), *Our New West* (1869), and *The Switzerland of America* (1869).

such great numbers might paralyse industry by furnishing suddenly a greater supply of labor than there will be demand for. I am going to try to attract them toward the hidden wealth of our mountain ranges, where there is room enough for all. Immigration, which even the war has not stopped, will land upon our shores hundreds of thousands more per year from overcrowded Europe. I intend to point them to the gold and silver that waits for them in the far West.

"Tell the miners for me, that I shall promote their interests to the utmost of my ability, because their prosperity is the prosperity of the nation, and," said he, his eyes kindling with enthusiasm, "we shall prove in a very few years that we are indeed *the treasury of the world.*"

Here I can hear you saying: "Where did you find these words of Lincoln?" I have just translated them literally from a speech given by Mr. Colfax before the miners of Central City on May 27, 1865.[4] You see that we are not the only ones to have had meetings with these bold pioneers of the Rocky Mountains, and that the president of the legislative assembly in Washington himself preceded us in that enterprise.

The evening of that same day, April 14, 1865, Mr. Colfax returned to the White House and found Lincoln leaving for the theatre. Lincoln invited Colfax to accompany him. Having other engagements for the evening, and on the eve of leaving Washington the following day, Mr. Colfax was unable to accept the invitation. As the President crossed the threshold of the White House, he clasped the traveler's hand.

"Do not forget, Colfax," he said, "our conversation of today. Tell those miners what I said to you today for them. Have a good trip! I shall send you a telegram at San Francisco. Farewell!"[5]

Such was the last farewell of Lincoln, and the last words he uttered on the affairs of the country; perhaps less than an hour later the

[4] Since Simonin translated directly from the Central City *Miners' Register* of June 1, 1865, which reported Lincoln's speech, the version that appeared there has been substituted for a translation from the French. The only phrase omitted by Simonin was "that the rebellion is overthrown." He also clarified certain references; for example, for Lincoln's "I am going to encourage that," he wrote, "I am going to encourage our underground explorations."

[5] The story of Colfax's visit to Lincoln on the night of the President's assassination is told in the *National Encyclopedia of American Biography* (New York: James T. White, 1897), IV, 13.

former comedy actor John Booth killed him point-blank, with a pistol shot, in a proscenium loge of the Ford Theatre.

And now I shall not say farewell, as did the martyr President to Mr. Colfax, but *au revoir*. I return tomorrow to Denver and from there to Cheyenne. That city was scarcely born at the time of my arrival on the prairies, a month ago. Today it has 3,000 inhabitants. A month ago the Pacific railroad ended at Julesburg; today it has reached Cheyenne, which is 140 miles farther West, at the very foot of the Rocky Mountains. I must go salute these marvels, see how cities and railroads spring up in the United States, and from there go pay my compliments to the Redskins of Dakota, the Sioux, the Crows, the Gros Ventres.

Tourists of the Mediterranean used to say, "See Naples and then die!" I, a humble excursionist on the prairies of the Far West, say, "See the Redskins and get scalped, but at least see the Redskins!"

CHAPTER 9

The Birth of a City

Cheyenne, territory of Dakota, at the end of the prairies, 1 November

We left yesterday morning from Denver by the Overland stage and in the most beautiful weather in the world. The coach was full, inside and out, not with baggage but with travelers. We were nine in the interior, three in each row; I leave you to judge what torture.

I had beside me a reverend of considerable size who was leaving Colorado, where he had not been successful, to go to Chicago to direct a journal and a printing establishment belonging to the sect which he represented.[1]

In front of me was a German engineer, of a corpulence no less formidable, who was just returning to Wisconsin to take up the direction of important zinc mines, after having just made a mineralogic tour of some months in the Rocky Mountains.

Need I mention my other companions? You know them in part: Colonel Heine, Mr. Whitney. A third was a journalist from Central City, owner of mines in Colorado and inventor of a new process for the treatment of gold-bearing sulphurs. Who here has not invented his own little process? He is headed toward the eastern states to turn his

[1] The portly reverend may be identified by the following item in the *Cheyenne Leader* of November 2, 1867: "Reverend J. B. McClure, recently pastor of the First Presbyterian Church at Denver, called on us yesterday morning. He is on his way to Chicago to assume the position of associate editor of the Northwestern Presbyterian, at that place."

discovery to advantage, to form a company. In America people cover 2,000 leagues on the slightest pretext.

This time we left our firearms with our baggage. No Indian raiders on this route. Under the October moon, peace was solemnly signed in Kansas by the commissioners of the Union with the five great nations of the South: the Apaches, Kiowas, Comanches, Arapahos, Cheyennes.[2] We may travel and sleep peacefully on the great desert route, across the country of the high grass. Praise be to the Manitou, the Great Spirit!

At La Porte (another French-Canadian name spared by American geography), we left the Overland Mail to follow its own route toward the country of the Mormons, those happy polygamists, and from there to the wild state of Nevada with its inexhaustible silver mines, and so to fertile California.[3] A supplementary stage came for the travelers whose destination was Cheyenne and the eastern states. Most of us were of this latter number, for we have left to another time our visit to the Latter Day Saints. The Mormon leader, Brigham Young, while we were still in Colorado, had written that he expected us.

What beautiful weather we had for this journey of a hundred miles across the great plains! It took us twenty-four hours. The sky was without a cloud, as it had been for a whole month before. No mist veiled the transparent atmosphere, and the air was exceptionally light, as is natural at these altitudes. The temperature was springlike, and a magnificent picture unrolled before our eyes all along the way.

---

[2] In October, 1867, representatives of the Kiowa, Comanche, Arapaho, Southern Cheyenne, and Apache tribes met with United States peace commissioners and agreed to accept reservations in Indian Territory, to respect the new railroad, and to accept from the U.S. government agencies, schools, agricultural guidance, clothing, and provisions, in return for the promise of eventual U.S. citizenship. The two resulting Medicine Lodge treaties are recorded in *Indian Affairs: Laws and Treaties* (Washington: G.P.O., 1904), Vol. II.

[3] La Porte, originally a camp site of French-Canadian trappers and hunters, became a town site in 1860. It was at one time headquarters for the Overland Stage Company.

The main Overland stage route did not go to Cheyenne, but north by way of Virginia Dale, Fort Sanders, Laramie Plains, and Fort Halleck, and then west to Salt Lake City.

The Birth of a City

The profile of the Rocky Mountains offers an enchanting view. To the south, Pikes Peak lifts its snowy summit to the clouds to a height of more than 4,200 metres, preserving the name of the celebrated explorer, Captain Pike, who first measured it in 1806.

To the north, Longs Peak, christened in 1820 by another hardy traveler, Colonel Long, lifts its no less picturesque peak to the same altitude. The two peaks are separated by a distance of 170 miles, yet the eye can take them in at the same time.[4]

Seen from a certain angle, Longs Peak shows two separate points; hence the name Peak of Two Ears given it by the old *coureurs* of the prairies, the trappers and Canadian traders who have frequented these areas since the 17th century, and certainly discovered before Captain Pike and Colonel Long the peaks which have immortalized their names. From whatever bank of the Missouri or the Mississippi one comes, after one has advanced some hundreds of miles on the prairies, he cannot fail to discover one or the other of these peaks, often both at the same time. One is, indeed, oriented by these mountains, as the sailor is by the North Star.

Between these two peaks is Mount Lincoln, higher even than the preceding ones and higher than our Mont Blanc, since, it is said, it exceeds 5,000 metres. Mount Lincoln was so named in honor of the martyred President, who did not need this christening to preserve a name pure above all for the most distant renown.[5]

This magnificent line of mountains is the most beautiful in North America. In Colorado, where it cuts along the meridian, it rises through the transparent and limpid atmosphere like an undulating mass of blue and violet hues, recalling the Apennines. Even so, the skyline of the peninsular range, though sung by Horace and many another poet, has not the thrilling aspect of this part of the Rocky Mountains, composed wholly of sharp granites of schists in deformed beds. The sky

[4] Pikes Peak (14,110 feet) was named in honor of Zebulon Montgomery Pike, and Longs Peak (14,255 feet), for Stephen H. Long. The distance between them is nearer 125 miles.

[5] Mount Lincoln refers to Mount Evans, renamed in 1870 for Governor John Evans of Colorado. Mount Evans is actually only 14,226 feet, or approximately 4,300 metres, high. No peak in the Rocky Mountains exceeds 4,400 metres.

of Colorado also recalls Italy. Everyone makes these comparisons, and the European traveler thinks himself near his own land, though 3,000 leagues separate him from it.

After such a fine day and such pleasant impressions, what an awakening we had! Pascal said, "Truth on this side the Pyrenees, error on that." We might have said as we arrived at the end of our road, "Fine weather on this side in Colorado, storm on the other!" This morning as we arrived in Cheyenne, on this plateau of more than 2,000 metres in altitude, we encountered a veritable cyclone as though in mid-ocean. The wind from the mountains had passed over their icy summits. It was as cold as winter, blew with a frightful violence, and lifted the gritty sand in thick clouds from the prairie. After November the season changes sharply here, and about every three days gusts of wind mixed with snow come up suddenly. Then the sun shines once more, and the sky resumes the summer azure transparence.

We inquired at Dodge House, or, if you prefer, Hotel, where we were offered lodging in the common sleeping room, if we were tired.[6] There, there were no less than thirty beds, most of them occupied by two sleepers at a time. The democratic customs of the Far West permit this nocturnal fraternity, and the American endures it with good grace.

We found it more convenient not to share a bed with anyone; but in the common lounging room, where everyone made his toilet, one had to make use of the same brushes, the same combs, and, yes, even the same towel. I rolled the soiled linen, spotted with dingy stains, until I found a clean place, and then bravely rubbed my face. What could I do? As they say in Spanish: *Es la costumbre del pais*, It is the custom of the country; and one should accept it like everyone else, for it would be tactless to pretend delicacy here.

The tavern keeper of Dodge House, who distributes ale and whiskey to his numerous customers, asked us to leave our arms. Rifles and revolvers are not permitted in the open in the city, under penalty of a

---

[6] Advertised in the *Cheyenne Leader* as early as September 19, 1867, was Dodge House, corner of O'Neill and Eighth streets, "J. H. Gildersleeve, Prop." A news item tells of "his amiable lady" and of the "cuisine" under the charge of Mr. Bell and his lady, formerly of Denver.

severe fine, a decision arrived at by the city council of Cheyenne after several recent brawls. Furthermore, the offenders were expelled for having troubled the public peace and created a scandal in this city born but yesterday. Bravo! And the result is that one can go about without arms, and walks in the midst of honest folk. And note that for this one has to come to the end of the prairies, to the foot of the Rocky Mountains, 520 miles west of the Missouri!

Everywhere I hear the sound of the saw and the hammer; everywhere wooden houses are going up; everywhere streets are being laid out, cut on the square, and not at oblique angles as in Europe. There is no time to hunt for names for these streets. They are street number 1, 2, 3, 4, or A, B, C, D, etc.

How happy the shade of Fénelon would be if it could pass this way! He dreamed of an ideal city, Salente. This is it, Cheyenne, the magic city, the wonder of the desert, as the pioneers have already called it, and not the windy city, as one of the travelers said this morning as he left us on his way to the eastern states.

Such is Cheyenne: it did not exist this last July, and the Indians from whom it took its name were camping in the neighborhood. They were still scalping the whites, for example, two soldiers from Fort Russell, two miles distant, whom they found one day alone, defenseless, and whom they killed without pity.

At the end of July a company was organized to build the city. At the same time a mayor and a municipal council were named. What name should they give to the city about to be born? Obviously, the name of the Indians of the region, for will that not soon be all that remains of the Redskins in these settled prairies?

There you have the modern Salente. Already stores are everywhere, especially of ready-made clothing, restaurants, hotels, saloons. To clothe oneself, eat, drink, and sleep, says the American, such are the four necessities which must be provided for in all newborn settlements. Already there are two printing shops, two newspapers, book shops, banks, stagecoaches, then the post office and the telegraph, to carry life and movement far away. And how many inhabitants has this city just sprung from the earth? More than 3,000. It has added a thousand inhabitants each month, and the railroad has not yet caught up with

63

it. The last station on the great Pacific railroad is Hillsdale, twenty miles to the east of Cheyenne; but already the diggers and bridge-builders are here. Cheyenne has not been forgotten; it has only gone on ahead (Go ahead!), preceding the railroad so as not to be forgotten when it passes.[7]

Houses arrive by the hundreds from Chicago, already made, I was about to say, all furnished, in the style, dimensions, and arrangements you might wish. Houses are made to order in Chicago, as in Paris clothes are made to order at the Belle Jardinière. Enter. Do you want a palace, a cottage, a city or country home; do you want it in Doric, Tuscan, or Corinthian; of one or two stories, an attic, Mansard gables? Here you are! At your service!

Only inhabitants are lacking, you might say, because they are not for sale; but they are coming. From the states of the Missouri and the Mississippi, even from Colorado, that young territory, the great exodus begins once more. *Allons*, let us go, pioneers, another step forward, another step with the sun! All over Colorado we have encountered the trains of hardy emigrants along all the roads. Men, women, children, with all their belongings, all the tools of a settler, were arriving in covered wagons drawn by heavy oxen or long-eared mules. The train was moving slowly, often followed by a cart loaded with planks, the embryo of the future home. Cheyenne has had its "excitement," and for a time Colorado feared that it might be depopulated by this city of the compelling attractions.

How rough and crude in appearance all these men of the Far West are, with their long hair, their broad-brimmed felt hats, their ill-kept beards, their clothing of nondescript color, their great leather boots engulfing their pantaloons! But at the same time what virile characters, proud, fearless! What dignity, what patience! No one complains here.

---

[7] The *Cheyenne Leader* of September 19, 1867, in its "Salutatory," speaks of Cheyenne as arising "scarce 6 weeks ago," and the "town where now between one and two hundred houses stand." By November 2 the paper claimed that "4,000 people are already settled here." The Union Pacific track, which Simonin says on November 1 is within twenty miles, reached Cheyenne on November 13, and was greeted the next day with a flowery editorial describing the astonishing speed of construction as men and machinery moved through Cheyenne with each step prepared and coordinated with a fine precision.

The Birth of a City

If things are not better, it is because that is impossible, and no one finds anything therein to blame.

Let us look about this city of three months, already so alive, so animated. Here are houses changing places, traveling down the streets borne on heavy vehicles. Dissatisfied with their first choice of location, they are going to locate elsewhere. The inhabitants have not even left their homes, and you see the sheet-iron chimney still smoking while the house moves along. But I have already witnessed this spectacle in New York and in San Francisco. Let us go on.

Here is the Ford restaurant, the "Véfour" of the place.[8] It does all the business you could wish, up to $1,000 a day. Just calculate it. Meals are a dollar, five francs. Three meals a day are served, and each time two to three hundred persons are seated at the different tables, not to mention the profits at the bar, the extras, etc.

There are plenty of other restaurants in Cheyenne, but Ford's leads them all. There are also those places pompously called parlors, salons, offices, where one goes to drink, usually standing, the sparkling ale or the alcoholic whiskey. I do not speak of the gaming halls, very much frequented and open especially at night. In some spots music attracts the customers, usually a large-sized Barbary [barrel] organ, playing operatic airs with full orchestration. These instruments are shipped in from Germany to all the saloons of any importance in the Far West. Germans are numerous here; they hear their native music, they enter.

Some saloons amuse their customers with other "attractions." Here is a gigantic diorama; here a painting by a master, in which you see Colonel Corcoran leading the brave under fire, or, if you prefer, the gallant 69th.

The newspapers have already announced our arrival.[9] It is not every day that a Parisian passes through Cheyenne, though that may

[8] Ford's restaurant, located on Sixteenth Street, was advertised thus in the October 10, 1867, *Leader*: "This house is fitted up regardless of expense, is clean and free from dust." The editor added his word on Mr. B. L. Ford, the proprietor: "As a caterer in his line Mr. Ford has no superior in the western country. We speak from personal knowledge."
The Véfour was a fashionable restaurant in Paris.
[9] See Appendix, pp. 162–163.

happen later. Let us thank these polite editors. In Cheyenne (as we had already seen at Georgetown in Colorado), the journalist is at once his own writer, compositor, proofreader, printer, and business manager, and sums up all these functions under the generic name of editor. The *Argus*, like the *Leader*, gives us a friendly reception. They kindly and freely offer us a copy of the day's issue. This costs fifteen cents at the shops. Announcements in particular fill these sheets, now of restricted dimensions, but to be expanded tomorrow. The different items are amusing.

"Charles Bell has brought a supply of apples from the Mormons. Charley has presented the editor of the *Leader* with some of these apples. Blessings on Charley Bell. The apples are excellent. They are the first fruit we have eaten in Cheyenne. We hope this bell will ring often."

"Yesterday," says a bookseller, who is at the same time a news dealer, a cigar and toy merchant, "Yesterday a certain person came into my shop. He unfolded everything and read everything, the *Monthly Magazine*, the *New York Herald*, and the *Chicago Tribune*, not to mention the *Leader* and the *Argus* of Cheyenne. He unfolded them all and read them all; and then he left without a word, without even thank you. Shame on the beggar!"

"Tomorrow," adds a reverend, "I shall celebrate the divine service in the saloon which Mr. A. has so kindly put at my disposal. We have as yet no church, but that will come before long. In the meantime, those who come tomorrow and who have prayer books will do well to bring them." [10]

[10] The *Cheyenne Leader* for November 2, 1867, ran this item: "Charley Bell has just received a big lot of fine apples fresh from Utah's umbrageous orchards. He has our thanks for a sample lot."

On November 5 the *Leader* carried the following under "Local Affairs": "We have to mention a case of cool impudence which occurred at a prominent news store in this city, Sunday morning. A man came in, stepped up to the counter, and taking up a copy of the LEADER, entertained himself in its complete perusal, inside and out, letter list and all, and returning it to the counter, sauntered away without as much as saying 'Thank you.' Gentlemen, come up and subscribe for it, at once; and get the additional comfort of the knowledge of having paid for it, as you read and contemplate the effect for your edification."

A search of the *Leader* did not uncover the reverend's announcement. Unfortunately, the *Argus* files have been destroyed, so it is impossible to determine whether the *Argus* ran the items as Simonin gives them, or whether the French visitor embellished them.

The Birth of a City

So goes the world. This little city, the youngest though not the least populated of all the cities of the world, which no geography yet mentions, proud of its hotels, its newspapers, its marvelous growth, its topographic situation, already dreams of the title of capital. It does not want to be annexed to Colorado, it wants to annex Colorado. As it is the only city in Dakota, and the territory is still completely untouched, it does not even wish to be a part of Dakota. It dreams of detaching a fragment from this territory and from Colorado and Utah, which it will call Wyoming, and of which it will be the center.[11] So is local patriotism born; and so local questions begin, even in the midst of the great desert. Every day the leading citizens of Cheyenne are full of these debates in the *Leader* and the *Argus,* and the discussion grows bitter with the newspapers of Denver and Central City, which respond haughtily, calling Cheyenne the windy city or the city of straw. If Denver were not so far, who knows what revolver shot might not be heard on one side or the other to back up these paper arguments?

This city pleases me, and I am sorry not to be able to spend the night here; but nowhere is there a bed available, even in the communal sleeping houses. I throw this letter in haste into the mail, and take off for Fort Russell[12] with my good companion, Colonel Heine (Mr. Whitney returned to Boston this morning). The Colonel knows certain former companions in arms at the fort, and we shall surely find a tent to live in for a few days.

Then we are going to see the Redskins of Dakota, with the Indian peace commission which meets at Fort Laramie to treat with the northern tribes as it has done with those of the South. To travel to the end of the prairies without seeing the savages, would that not be like going to Rome without seeing the Pope?

[11] And Cheyenne succeeded. Since 1868 an act of Congress decrees the forming of this territory of Wyoming. [*Simonin's note.*]

[12] Fort D. A. Russell, now Fort Francis E. Warren, was established in the spring of 1867 by General Grenville M. Dodge and was named in honor of Brigadier General David A. Russell. It is located approximately two or three miles northwest of Cheyenne.

CHAPTER 10

The Soldiers of the Desert

Fort Russell (Dakota), under the tent, 1 November

The most cordial hospitality awaited us here, and with pleasure we exchanged the communal sleeping room of Dodge House for the soldier's tent.

General Stevenson,[1] who commands the fort, the major, the quartermaster, the officers, all have received us as friends. We have sat at their "mess," we have toasted one another, and drunk the sacramental glass of whiskey without which no good acquaintance is made in the United States. We have been received with all possible honors. A sentinel watches over our tent; in the evening we answer his call to return to our quarters.

The bad weather has continued. The day before yesterday a terrible tempest of snow came up suddenly. On the way from the General's tent to our own we almost, like Romulus, disappeared in the midst of the storm. The roof of our tent was frozen, and snow covered the edge of my bed where it touched the canvas.

Then the fine weather returned, and, while awaiting the Indian peace commission, we went hunting the wild cocks of the desert, near the fort along a stream bordered with water birch. There are no more bison or antelope here since the soldiers have come and the Pacific railroad has sent its tracklayers and rail-workers into these regions.

---

[1] General John Dunlap Stevenson (1821–1897) followed General C. C. Augur as second commandant of Fort D. A. Russell.

The Soldiers of the Desert

Nothing remains of the prairie save its characteristic flora, especially the high grasses from which it derives its name, now dried and yellow. The alluvial soil remains as distinctive, too, composed here of thick earth on which you find not a stone, though sometimes also of siliceous gravels and round pebbles. These must have descended from the Rocky Mountains at a time when they were uplifted, or when the glaciers which in former geologic ages rested on the flanks of these high mountains were suddenly melted. These gravels and rounded pebbles, including those in the living streams, are specimens collected in profusion by nature at that same time, as if to indicate in advance what rocks will be found by the geologist who is headed for the great chain of the extreme West.

Here one sees pebbles of rose granite, green porphyry, glossy and foliated slate, and quartz of all colors, especially the red quartz with which the beds of some streams are paved.

The only rock found in place on the prairie is the soft sandstone, quite modern in age, whose stratifications, worked upon and disintegrated by the elements, sometimes offer very curious spectacles even, when the extent of the strata is considerable, resembling ruined cities. It is these rocks, or accumulations of rounded pebbles, which generally form the modest knolls which are called "bluffs," and which give the prairie that undulating appearance which has caused the Americans to speak of the "rolling prairies."

The red quartzes, descended from the flanks of the Rocky Mountains and disintegrated by running water into tiny particles, in several places form the subsoil of the prairie. In these spots, the ants sometimes pile up enormous hillocks of these gravels around their nests, more than two feet in height and twelve or fifteen in circumference. What are the pyramids of Egypt beside these?

These deposits of siliceous and ferruginous gravels, whether excavated or not by ants, are so widespread in certain regions, especially those which extend to the east and north of Colorado Territory and over a part of the Pacific railroad, as to give these regions the name of the Great American Desert. In other areas of the prairie the soil exhibits another phenomenon: the waters are so saturated with alkali, or carbonate of soda, that it is deposited in a whitish efflorescence on the surface of the terrain. One of the stations of the Pacific railroad bears the significant name of Alkali. Pity the man or beast who drinks of these waters! Needless to add that the soil in these places is entirely sterile, for the young plants are burned by the salt. Certain areas of the great American desert are strewn with alkaline lands, and seem in the center and south of the prairies to be a continuation of what are called in the north the Bad Lands, so widespread in Dakota and Nebraska. In all these localities the relief or configuration of the soil is otherwise the same, for in the Bad Lands one meets with the same considerable stretches of knolls of soft sandstone resembling ruined buildings.

A journey across the prairies is far from being monotonous, and everyone, hunter or naturalist, can glean something there. No doubt the tourist who now takes the Pacific railroad goes too fast to enjoy to the full the great spectacle of the Far West; but once arrived at the last station, he travels as before by caravan, protected by God and his revolver. What will replace these poetic journeys, the halts in the tall grass, when there is no other fuel for cooking the meal than the dung of the bison, the cow chips, as the trappers call it? What will replace the long evening meditations when the only shelter is the tent on the native grass, under the star-studded sky, where nothing obstructs the horizon, and where, free and independent, with no master but oneself, one finds himself alone, face to face with vast nature?

The prairie level climbs imperceptibly from the banks of the Missouri to the Rocky Mountains. Omaha is 300 metres above the ocean's waters; Cheyenne, 515 miles from Omaha, is close to 2,000 metres. The Pacific railroad has happily profited by this natural grade.

The climate in all these regions is in summer one of the finest in North America. The elevation above sea level does not wholly prevent a somewhat excessive heat, but the breezes which come from the Rocky Mountains soon cool the atmosphere. It never rains. Toward the end of autumn the climate is sometimes rigorous, as I have discovered at my own expense; but after a storm of several days, the sky often returns serene, without a single cloud to veil it.

In winter the same successions of good and bad weather occur; snow falls in abundance, but does not remain for long. The cold is sometimes bitterly felt, and the thermometer sometimes reaches the readings of Siberia, twenty-five and thirty degrees below zero, centigrade. In summer it occasionally climbs to the heat of Senegal, and so the extremes are found together.

During the entire year the atmosphere is exceptionally pure and dry, at the same time very thin and light. Butchered meat keeps quite safely in the open air. Animals remain loose outside without any shelter. It is a climate particularly favorable to delicate persons, especially in the spring and summer; they regain their strength in this refreshing dry air, or, if they come ill to the prairies, return cured after one season. A bath of fresh air in such cases is worth much more than a mineral bath and produces more certain results.

Such are the chief characteristics of the great American desert, from which I write you at this moment. While awaiting the peace commission, I am living among soldiers who scarcely resemble those of our country.

Some of the officers have studied at West Point, the Saint-Cyr of the United States; others are soldiers of fortune who took up the musket in the War of Secession, and who have preferred to remain soldiers rather than become lawyers or merchants like so many others. In all of them one meets with the greatest civility and the most polished and civilized manners, which happily temper military rigidity.

There is a library at the fort, but no one reads much. More often they hunt, play billiards, or drink. The commandant mingles the practice of business with the profession of arms. He has bought what they call a "corner lot" in Cheyenne, one of those sites which touch on two streets at once, like those so preferred by the wine merchants of Paris. I leave you to guess how sought after these lots are in Cheyenne and elsewhere. In all these newly founded towns there is competition to have one, and men gamble and speculate over them.

General Stevenson, not content with these lots, has also contrived to erect a vast storehouse in Cheyenne, a regular warehouse in stone, if you please, and not in wood. He hopes to store merchandise there from one or another source, when the Pacific railroad has united the two seas and has developed into the great commercial highway of the world. Every day the General, in his "buggy" drawn by two smart horses, visits his growing estates and calculates like Perette[2] how much they will bring him.

---

[2] Perette, the milkmaid in La Fontaine's tale, calculated her income from the milk, tossed her head, and spilled all the milk.

Like Perette, too, he came near seeing all his dreams vanish the other day, not because he broke his jug of milk, but because on his return from Cheyenne his horses ran away and the General was thrown to the bottom of his vehicle and was all but left on the road.

The glass of whiskey has its numerous devotees here, for what can one who does not drink do in the desert? Each officer is the owner of a little chest with compartments which he carries with him on his travels. You might take it for a chest of books, the library of an amateur tourist. In it glasses and flasks are skillfully arranged. "Will you take a drink?" is the first word uttered, as soon as you enter the tent. It would be tactless to refuse. You say yes, and the "old Bourbon whiskey" of Kentucky is forthwith poured in your honor. The glasses go the rounds. What a bouquet, my friend, and what a treacherous liquor is this "old Kentuck!" Our old cognac is nothing in comparison. How many allow themselves to be captured by this taste, and how many partisans, in my opinion, this whiskey rates among American officers! If you would not be tempted, the best thing is not to taste it, as the monkey in the fable said, who, led on from one sugared almond to the next, ended by emptying the bag.

Some of the married officers have brought their wives with them. These courageous women have said farewell to New York or Boston and come without a word of complaint to join their husbands and children at the end of the desert. After all, they are only 1,000 leagues from their native soil.

The private soldier merits less praise than his officers. You know that the regular army in America in time of peace is reduced to almost nothing. There are scarcely 65,000 men at this moment to guard a country as vast as all central Europe; and furthermore, of these 65,000 one out of four deserts, as General Grant states in his most recent report.

These soldiers are for the most part scattered in certain Atlantic and Pacific forts, then in the forts, posts, and stations of the Far West, to keep the Indians in awe. Fort Russell conforms to this description; it is one of the main military posts of the United States, though a fort only in name, for, like most prairie forts, it has neither dungeons nor entrenchments. As for ramparts and the masterly constructions of military genius, these are everywhere absent. Of what use would they

72

be? There is no need for such arts against the Indian, and the Pacific railroad alone will do more against the Redskin than all the forts combined. The savage is best combated by the weapons of civilization.

How different is this regular army from our European troops, so thoroughly regimented and disciplined! These soldiers are from every country except the United States. They are Canadian, Irish, German, Belgian, French, men discharged from the Mexican legion, and all of them can say with certainty that the most curious thing about this cosmopolitan army is that they find themselves in it. All of them enlisted in the American army in the hope of soon becoming generals, and all have remained common soldiers. "My English is to blame," one of them, a discontented Breton, just now said to me; "this cursed English, I understand it, but I can't speak it."

Another, a Canadian who still speaks the French of the time of Louis XIV (otherwise not bad French), argued that he had never had anything but bad luck. He would prefer to serve somewhere else. He was born of a French mother, though his father was Scotch. A third, a Belgian who had come to the United States in the hope of making a quick fortune, had lost the little he had, and had enlisted, to find himself still a common soldier after fourteen years of service.

Nevertheless, all these soldiers of the desert, these pioneers of a new breed, bravely do their duty when the occasion demands. They have fought well against the Redskin in many encounters, and they too have played their part in the settlement of the Great Plains. But nothing can replace the volunteer, the free soldier of the territories or the armed citizen of the States, when the country is in danger. They are the true guardians of the nation, and remind me of the fine saying of Machiavelli that the breasts of citizens are the best frontiers of a nation.

In the conflict with the Redskins, in the midst of newborn territories, and in the great war which recently divided North and South, it was above all the brave volunteers who saved the Union.

We are told that the Indian peace commission will arrive tomorrow. It is composed of Mr. Taylor, commissioner of Indian affairs at Washington; Mr. Henderson, senator, president of the committee on Indian affairs of the Senate; Generals of the regular army Harney, Sherman, Terry; the general and the colonel of the Colorado volunteers, Sanborn and Tappan. Mr. White, attaché to the Indian Bureau in Washington, is the secretary of the commission, and Mr. Taylor its president.[3]

A draftsman, a stenographer, guides, interpreters, and divers agents accompany the commission, and, as you might suppose, some reporters from the newspapers of New York, Chicago, St. Louis, etc.

General Stevenson has already requisitioned the necessary number of covered wagons for the official caravan, and has selected eighty soldiers to serve as an escort. He also plans to assign a wagon to my companion and me, with the inevitable four mules and a mule driver.

Tomorrow morning we start for Hillsdale, the last station on the Pacific railroad, where we shall join the commission on its return from the southern tribes. From there, across the vast solitudes of the prairie and with no fear of an unfortunate encounter, since we have eighty soldiers with us, our long caravan will take the route to Fort Laramie. We shall need three days to arrive, trotting twelve hours a day and camping at night under the bright stars. The distance is not less than 100 miles.

At Fort Laramie we shall find the Crows, the Sioux, the Arapahos of the North, whom the commissioners have long since summoned for the rendezvous. At last we shall see the Redskins, not just two, man and wife, like those shown last summer at the Exposition, but whole tribes. We shall smoke the peace pipe with them, and ask them to give us theoretical lessons in the delicate art of scalping.

3 General William Tecumseh Sherman, commanding the Military Division of the Mississippi, was not among the commissioners to Fort Laramie as originally planned. His place was taken by General C. C. Augur, who, along with Major Generals William S. Harney and Alfred H. Terry, was a presidential appointee to the commission and advocated a policy of uncompromising severity toward the Indians. The congressional appointees to the commission, who favored compromise and opposed the use of force in dealing with the Indians, included Nathaniel Greene Taylor, Commissioner of Indian Affairs and a former Methodist minister; Senator John B. Henderson of Missouri, chairman of the Senate Committee on Indian Affairs; Samuel F. Tappan of Colorado; and General John B. Sanborn. Ashton S. H. White served as secretary to the commission.

CHAPTER 11

A Caravan

Lone Tree Creek, Dakota, under the tent, 9 November

Three days ago, at an early hour, we left Fort Russell. The total expedition comprised some thirty wagons, drawn by 130 animals in all, thirty-five mule drivers and various agents, and finally our eighty soldiers. These latter rode in the wagons with all their camping equipment. At the head of the convoy the officers wheeled their horses about. The weather had again become frightful, as it sometimes does in autumn on these prairies, at an elevation of 2,000 metres. Since the first of the month, as I wrote you, a terrible storm accompanied by snow has passed over Fort Russell; and though the snow soon melted under the sun's rays, the storm, after a day or two of calm, began to blow like a veritable cyclone. The dust, raised in thick clouds, entered our wagons, which where open in the rear, literally blinding those within. The cold was biting; the thermometer hovered below the freezing point, for the wind from the Rocky Mountains had passed over their frozen summits.

Leaving Fort Russell in the morning under such conditions, we arrived toward afternoon at Hillsdale. This place will soon yield its title as last station on the Pacific railroad to Cheyenne, which in turn will soon cede it to its neighbor on the West.

Hillsdale lacked water and wood, and the prairie winds blew with what seemed an increasing violence. Furthermore, the commissioners who were supposed to arrive on the Pacific railroad had as yet given no sign. What to do? An artesian well was sunk along the way, close to the station, but the storm interfered with the operation, and we could only hope that a bit of water might be obtained to give some drink to our mules and horses.

The locality was depressing to see. Only a few saloons remained upright; everyone, moving west with the iron road, had emigrated to Cheyenne. It was thereupon decided that we should camp on the prairie, a few miles from Hillsdale. There, in a spot well known to caravans, we should find fresh water and wood, two indispensable things on the desert.

Lodgepole Creek (the stream of the lodgepole),[1] where we arrived toward four o'clock, was already occupied by the mule drivers who had left Fort Russell that morning, assigned to transport the gifts which the commissioners would present to the Indians. Our men ranged themselves beside the firstcomers. The soldiers quickly installed their tents, and soon the campfires were glowing in the night. The mule drivers dug a hole in the earth, lit their fires in it, and set up their stoves. Without losing any time they cooked the "flat-jacks" [*sic*], a sort of fritter or pancake, and the ham or bacon cut into slices, while at one corner of the fire an immense kettle contained tea or coffee, the customary drink with all American meals. The mule drivers are always the first and the best served, in these expeditions in the Great West, and our men had already finished their meal before the soldiers had scarce begun theirs, and before the head cook for the officers, to whose mess we were invited, had even set up his stove. True, it was a cast-iron and sheet-iron stove, and its installation alone, because of the raging wind, demanded more time than it took to cook the meal.

Sleeping, like the supper, left much to be desired. Our wagon served us as a shelter. A bearskin was our bed and a buffalo hide our cover. The baggage was disposed about the rear of the vehicle and protected us in part from the wind and the cold, but we slept none too well.

The scene from our camp was most picturesque. The mules, unharnessed, had been gathered in separate groups. They had soon exhausted their slender ration of corn, and grazed on the prairie grasses,

---

[1] Lodgepole Creek is two or three miles north of Hillsdale, which is itself some twenty-five miles east of Cheyenne.

now yellow with the autumn frosts. The wagons were lined up, forming a kind of rampart.

In the other direction, toward Lodgepole Creek, rose the soldiers' tents. At right angles were those of the officers. The water of the stream was frozen at the edges, and here and there, in tufted bunches along the banks, rose the water birch and the bushes. A natural talus of soft stone and alluvium formed one slope of the stream. Otherwise the vast plain stretched in all directions in slight undulations to the horizon. The sky was brilliant with stars, the moon shed its light on the prairie, and in the distance one heard the muffled barking of wolves or hungry coyotes. The last fires went out and the silence of the camp was broken only by the lingering step of some late watchman seeking his tent, or the whinny of some mule disputing a tuft of grass or the shelter of a wagon with its neighbor. Soon a great calm fell, and nothing was heard but the whistling of the wind in the solemnity of the night.

On the next day, the seventh of November, the sun rose on the Lodgepole Creek camp without bringing fair weather with it. The storm had even redoubled in violence. One saw wagons, with the force of the wind alone, move on their wheels for several metres. Some tents were thrown to the ground. Walking outside became impossible. On top of this bad luck, the commissioners did not arrive, and we had another long day to wait for them. Early yesterday morning we were finally notified of their arrival, and camp was lifted, to the great joy of everyone.

General Sherman and Senator Henderson, recalled to Washington by their duties and by the impending date of the opening of the legislative session, had not been able to join the commission though they were its principal members. General Sherman had been replaced by General Augur, commandant of the Platte area, with headquarters at Omaha. General Augur, like General Terry, another of the commissioners and commandant of the Dakota territory, is one of the officers who most distinguished himself in the War of Secession. Both joined to their deportment that practice of civil habits which so tempers military stiffness, and which creates a difference between the soldiers of the Union and those of other countries entirely in the favor of the first.

77

The aged General Harney, now become the best friend of the Redskins after having fought them without mercy, stands out among all the commissioners by his kindly, paternal manner. Despite his sixty-eight years, he agreed to take a most active part in all the tasks so unexpectedly entrusted to him. An old, retired military man, a veteran of the western forts, he never weakened for a moment, whether in the vicissitudes of the journey or the length of the councils. He invariably wore the general's uniform, and it was good to see this straight, proud soldier, with his moustache and white hair, still young despite his years. A faithful black, in a green livery and a pointed felt hat decorated with stripes and gold tassels, served him as a domestic and alone guarded his tent. Along with the General came the president of the commission, the honorable Mr. Taylor, commissioner of Indian affairs at Washington. Clad in a plain civilian costume, he showed in his features something of the clergyman, and by his placid, almost ministerial manner was well fitted to head the peace commission.

The general and the colonel of volunteers Sanborn and Tappan, who recently distinguished themselves in several encounters with the Indians of Colorado, had about them perhaps a more martial air than that of their colleagues, the generals of the regular army, thus indicating that the militia and the national guard are taken seriously in the United States.

Mr. White, secretary of the commission; Mr. Howland, painter;[2] Mr. Wallace, stenographer; and finally the "reporters" from certain newspapers of Saint Louis, Chicago, and New York represent the younger and noisier part of the expedition, and mingle their jokes with the graver discussion of the commissioners.

Everyone received the Parisian who asked the favor of accompanying the commission with the greatest affability, and soon I counted only friends in the company of so many persons who did not know me the night before. As soon as one is "introduced" to an American, as soon as one has clasped or "shaken" his hand, as they say, acquaintance is made, and the American becomes your friend. This is one of the attractive sides of the simple and democratic manners in the United States.

---

[2] This was undoubtedly "Captain Jack" Howland, who had started painting western scenes in 1859 and in about 1867 was in the Central City area. In later years he was a staff artist for *Harper's*.

A Caravan

The Canadian Leon Pallardy accompanied the commission as interpreter for the Sioux language.[3] At the same time, he served as guide for the three chiefs of the Sioux nation, Fast Bear, Swift Bear, and White Eyes. At least, these are the names by which the commissioners have agreed to recognize these sachems, for the first two have names absolutely untranslatable in our modest language. They could be written only in Latin, and even then!

The three chiefs wore as their sole clothing a blanket of wool and leggings with moccasins of leather. One did have trousers, but after the custom of the Redskins, he had cut out the rear. This one carried bow and arrows, which the plains warrior relinquishes so reluctantly; another held the peace pipe, which plays so large a role in all Indian deliberations. It is a pipe with a long red bowl, from which extends a stem of boxwood or cherrywood, decorated with nails of brass. A dozen smokers share the same pipe, each one taking a puff and handing the pipe to his neighbor.

Yesterday, as we were leaving, I approached these great chiefs. True to the habit of all Indians, who make it a rule never to show emotion, the Sioux remained impassive. I tried to engage them in conversation, but they spoke not a word of English. Crouched, wrapped in their blankets, they uttered only the word "Soux, Soux! Cold, cold!" which signified that they were Sioux and very cold, understandable enough in view of the temperature without and the way these poor fellows shivered.

Pallardy came up. "They are good savages," he said. "We brought them to Fort Laramie to show them to the others. Swift Bear is going to plow this winter, with his men. He has agreed to live on the reservation and cultivate the land. He is not very happy about it, but he likes the whites and wants to please them."[4]

[3] Captain Eugene F. Ware, in *The Indian War of 1864* (Lincoln: University of Nebraska Press, 1960), p. 202, described Pallardy thus: "Another of these guides and pioneers was Leo Palladie [*sic*]. He was a pure Frenchman, but of the blue-eyed type. He had curly hair, and the happiest disposition of any frontiersman. He was a reader of books and newspapers, and yet he was a thoroughgoing mountaineer. He spoke all the Indian languages in the neighborhood, was an adept at their sign language, was always good-natured, telling stories and having fun."

[4] Swift Bear, the leader of a band of Brulés, had long been friendly toward the whites.

This conversational opening soon broke the ice between Pallardy and me. The Canadian was delighted to see a compatriot, and I to travel with a man who knew the Sioux so well and was so well respected among them. Pallardy is small of stature, well proportioned, vigorous, with sharp features, and in every way illustrates the type of trader or prairie hunter as he is usually imagined.

"I had been married just eight days when the commission came to look for me," he told me. "I left my wife and the hotel I built in North Platte; it cost me all of seventy-five thousand francs [approximately fifteen thousand dollars]. I left all that to accompany the commission. I like the prairie life, which brings back my first occupation of trader. I have been to the *city* (as the traders call St. Louis) no more than three times in twenty years. I was sick when I went. I have built a beautiful buffet at the railroad station in North Platte, where the train stops. Come to see me when you go through. I'll introduce you to my wife; she cried a lot when I left."

Eventually our long caravan left the Lodgepole Creek camp and started across the endless prairie. The wagons went in single file. At the head, on horseback, rode the officers who commanded the convoy, then came the vehicles of the different members of the commission, and after them the wagons of those who had attached themselves to the expedition by duty or out of curiosity. Among these were the reporters of the eastern papers, certain relatives or friends of the commissioners, Pallardy with his three sachems, an army commissary going to sell beef at Fort Laramie, and several other "excursionists." Also along was an intruder who had slipped into the convoy, whom no one knew, and who had followed the commission for a month under pretext of "making some business," but cursing the bad weather, the slowness of the mules, the lack of supplies, and the poor quality of the food. Yet so great is American patience and such the respect for the individual that no one rebuked this man or dreamed of sending him packing. Finally, at the rear of the caravan, came the soldiers' wagons and the wagons carrying trunks and provisions. The mule drivers took pains to keep their positions and whipped their beasts vigorously, with strong oaths, if they threatened to slow their steps.

We traveled thus yesterday the whole day, despite the cold and the raw wind, and in the afternoon arrived at Horse Creek, where we camped to eat and spend the night, for there, there ran a stream of fresh water, and there was an abundance of wood. The camp was sheltered by a bluff of stalactites, a witness to the incrustating springs which once watered these regions. The rock had been little by little decomposed by the weather, and the ground was covered with a thick siliceous sand.[5]

Today we broke camp early and set out more cheerfully than yesterday, for the storm had finally ceased, and the cold had yielded to a more clement temperature.

The place where we are camped this evening is the most picturesque of the Far West. It is called Lone Tree Creek.[6] Picture a rampart of sandstone crowning a vast plateau of jagged rocks worn down by the elements, rain, wind, ice, and snow, and that continuously since the era when the rocks were deposited a thousand centuries ago. In such manner they have taken on strange and captivating forms by which the eye itself is deceived. Here is a tower in ruins, there a long wall with more than one open breach. Farther on is a gate opening into the city which is protected by these fortresses; and above them a human form seems to watch, a guard ready to give the alarm. And the illusion persists, for opposite is another plateau topped by the same walls, the same bastions. They look like rival cities, with only the deep valley between them. Halfway up grow dwarfed cedars and cypresses whose dark outlines from afar resemble the yawning mouths of so many caves dug into the walls to topple them.

These are the "Scott's Bluffs," so named, no doubt, in memory of the trapper who first saw them.[7] They stretch over immense distances,

[5] The Horse Creek camp site must have been near where Highway 85 crosses that stream today.

[6] The Lone Tree camp site may be reached easily today by leaving Highway 85 some three miles south of Hawk Springs and turning west on a good graveled highway leading to Chugwater. Some seven miles straight west, at the point of the first curve of the present road south and again west, to climb the ridge, an old, unimproved trail proceeds slightly north of west to the mouth of the Lone Tree Creek canyon. At this same point, the old trail crossed the present highway on its way northwest to the small stream where Simonin and his party camped.

[7] Simonin is in error here. Scotts Bluff was located on the south side of the Platte River, in present-day Scotts Bluff County, Nebraska. The Lone Tree Creek camp was very slightly east of due south of Fort Laramie.

These rock formations, which Simonin identifies as sandstone, are, according to Dr. Samuel H. Knight, University of Wyoming geologist, Arikaree sandstone above Brule clay, the latter made up in large part of altered volcanic ash, hence the whiteness of the rocks.

and long before we arrived at the camp we had perceived them on the horizon. The sky was partially clouded, some black clouds disputing with the sun for a place. The sun played thus with the clouds, now highlighting and now darkening the bluffs, so that the gray stone ramparts seemed now whitened with snow, and now about to disappear entirely in the shadows. This optical effect, repeated at regular intervals, was astonishing; and none could turn his eyes from the magnificent spectacle. The view changed further as we gradually approached, and by the time we arrived at the foot of the bluffs it was a wholly different thing. The mule drivers halted their animals of their own accord, and each remained for some seconds silent in awe. Some compared these geologic ruins to the most ancient cities of Asia; others recalled the Flood. History and fable took turns, and the discussion continued the more lively as we drew alongside these marvelous rocks to the spot we had picked for our camp. Here a complete wall surrounded the plain, interrupted only by the narrow passage opened by the Lone Tree Creek, and gave at once protection against the wind and the Indians.

These natural walls of soft sandstone, which still recalled, even close at hand, the ruins of ancient cities, are not uncommon on the prairies. Their extent is truly considerable over the territory which we have covered, and occupies a circle of perhaps fifty or sixty miles in circumference, though, it is true, with very long breaks in the continuity. In Colorado the rocks of Monument Creek and the Garden of the Gods, and in Nebraska those of the Bad Lands, are of the same type. It was, no doubt, these ruins of a new kind which stimulated the minds of the first trappers to those legends of ancient cities, no longer inhabited but to be found in the midst of the prairies, their walls and fortresses still upright, legends which circulated for a long time among the emigrants of the Far West.

From Lone Tree Creek a new stretch will take us tomorrow directly to Fort Laramie, between morning and evening. We shall pause only toward midday to let the mules drink and rest a moment, while we have our "lunch." We shall arrive at the fort before night, after having covered a distance of 100 miles, or 160 kilometres, from Lodgepole Creek, in three days. The route we have followed is well known to traders and old trappers. It was pointed out to the commission by Pallardy, who

Building the Union Pacific Railroad, Western Nebraska, 1867

A Denver Street (F Street)

View of Central City
From Le tour du monde, 1868.

Georgetown in the 1860's

Pikes Peak

From Le tour du monde, *1868.*

Courtesy of the Wyoming State Archives and Historical Department

Cheyenne, 1867

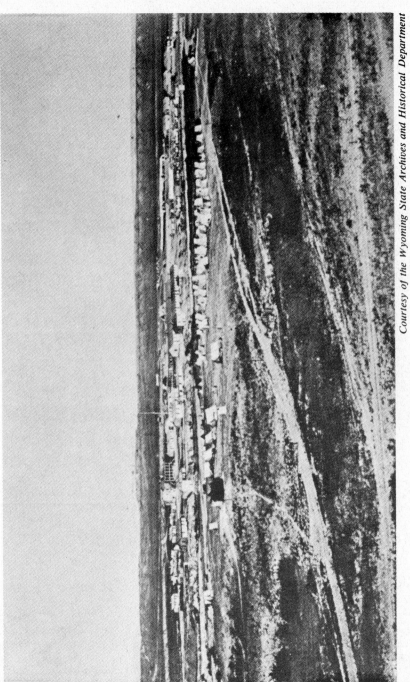

Courtesy of the Wyoming State Archives and Historical Department

Fort Laramie, ca. 1870

Photograph by W. H. Jackson.

Courtesy of the Wyoming State Archives and Historical Department

From left to right: Pierre Richard, his Sioux wife, an unidentified Indian, and
a trader or hunter

himself often made use of it a few years back, when he was trading with the Indians.

"That was a good time," he said to me just now. "In the autumn all the savages, Sioux, Blackfeet, Crows, Gros Ventres, came together on the Lone Tree Creek plateau, right where we camped. You could have a buffalo robe or several beaver skins, for a cup of sugar, a package of smoking tobacco. The savage was a good fellow, we liked one another, and we made lots of money.

"Today the whites have come, the bison has left or disappeared. The Indians mistrust us, and we have turned bad. You pay ten or twenty dollars for a buffalo robe, five dollars for a beaver skin, and business is no good any more."[8]

What would Pallardy have thought if he had been able to transport himself suddenly to those primitive times when only a few rare trappers knew the prairie, or when a trader went in the same year, without ceremony, from Mexico or Louisiana to Canada? This was often to exchange products of the soil for furs; and sometimes also just "to chat a little in the city," as was the case with the French, who traveled several hundred miles from the end of the prairies to New Orleans, or from the Great Lakes to St. Louis, for this purpose.

The route which these *coureurs* of the prairies followed still bears the name among the Americans of the Spanish Trail, as the Mexican or Spanish path was called. Fort Laramie is today the principal station on this route, situated at the confluence of the Laramie River with the North Platte, in a rolling prairie.[9] There tomorrow we shall salute the starry flag of the Union, and there the Americans will once again find their fatherland in the very heart of the desert.

---

[8] The prairie traders were once more numerous than now. They carried on a barter trade with the Indians and took buffalo hides and other furs and gave in return sugar, coffee, meal, tobacco, cloth, and blankets. Whiskey and arms were prohibited, but were nevertheless principal objects of exchange. Like all barter business, the traffic soon enriched the traders, who profited heavily on both sides. Great firms in St. Louis advanced funds for this commerce, and caravans set out in the good season of the year. The Indians were particularly tempted by powder and arms. Today it is still the first thing they ask of the commissioners of the Union when they meet in council with them. [*Simonin's note.*]

[9] Fort Laramie served as a fur-trade post and supply depot from 1834 until 1849 when it became a military post. It was an important point on the Oregon Trail.

CHAPTER 12

Fort Laramie

Fort Laramie, Dakota, 11 November

The fort where we are camped is one of the principal military posts of the West. It was built some thirty years ago on the very site of a trader's post for the fur trade carried on with the Indians by a great St. Louis firm, the Chouteau. Laramie, or Laramée, who gave his name to the fort and the region, was a Canadian hunter killed here by the Sioux while he was setting his beaver traps. This event took place toward 1830, and the whites kept the memory of it alive by linking the name of Laramie with the geography of the country. The name of Laramie has been bestowed on the river which passes the fort and joins the North Platte, and on the high peak some miles away, a landmark to the fact of the Rocky Mountains, as well as on the fort itself. Many a traveler, forgotten in the christenings of geography, has been less fortunate than this poor hunter.

Seen from the route we followed, the fort resembled more a Spanish-American village than a military post of the United States. The barracks, the warehouses, the offices, the officers' quarters, all are constructed of stone and whitewashed with lime. On one side of the large open space for maneuvers is the residence of the general in command of the fort. With its two-story "veranda," or outer gallery, one would take it for a hotel in Panama or Central America. Not far off is a building of a style even stranger for this country, a kind of Swiss chalet, which the "sutler," or supply merchant, of the post has built from his

84

own profits. The refinement of this dwelling puts to shame the mean appearance of the low, gloomy canteen. Beside the chalet rises the only tree to be seen about the fort. The new "barracks," or soldiers' quarters, and the storehouses are built of wood.

Along the Laramie River is the "corral," or pen, a large square enclosure surrounded by a fence. There the hay is kept and the mules enclosed. The angles of the corral on the side opposite the river are each defended by an octagonal structure of "adobe," or mud wall (bricks cooked in the sun). These defenses were originally built to resist the incursions of the Indians, who surprised emigrant trains or military posts by first of all seizing the mules and horses, so highly valued by them. Today the Indians are far away, and the corral forts have been transformed into mess halls for the mule drivers. Instead of iron weapons there are only kitchen utensils.

A wooden bridge on piles joined by swaying planks connects the two banks of the river. On the left bank is the fort with all its out-buildings; on the right bank, the one hotel of the region, where the officers have their mess. In winter, the big floods carry off the floor of the bridge, and then a boat anchored to the bank serves to carry the boarders across. The hotel is built of adobe and large wooden logs, like the "log house" of the American pioneer. It is but one story, but it is most comfortable for living and for meals, especially when one reflects that everything must be brought from the states, 500 or 600 miles away. Beside the hotel is the indispensable saloon, where chiefly ale and whiskey are sold. The dealer also sells books, as if to temper the effect of these drinks, though his customers apply themselves more frequently to his casks than to his library. True, the post office of the fort also competes with the latter by selling novels and newspapers in the intervals between the arrival and departure of the couriers. These take place only every two weeks, and are furthermore subject to the good will of Red Cloud and his band, or so the postmaster takes pains to announce on his bulletin board.

The residents of Fort Laramie number 500 or 600: officers, clerks, soldiers, army mule drivers. As at Fort Russell, some of the officers have studied at West Point, the military school of the United States, situated in the state of New York on the banks of the Hudson River.

Residence at Laramie is none too agreeable, and the climate is quite rigorous in winter, during which one often goes without news for several months. The boredom of this remote and isolated site is combated chiefly by hunting: on the prairies, the buffalo and antelope, the squirrel, and the wolf; in the mountains, deer, elk, the wildcat, and the bear, some species of which are very dangerous—these offer the hunter the excitement and danger he seeks. One finds elaborate trophies on some of the buildings, proofs of numerous victories. According to the custom, some married officers have brought their wives with them. Like all American women, they arrive in the desert without a word of complaint and mingle the sweet joys of family life with the rigors of enforced exile. As for the soldiers, they are as in all the army the sweepings of the population of the United States. Among them are the rebels of all countries, except true Americans.

The garrison of Fort Laramie comprises four companies of infantry and two of cavalry. We know how readily these soldiers desert. "As soon as I get a chance," said one of them, a Canadian who spoke the old French, "I shall skip out." All of them are discontented and quarrel with their comrades. None is content except Macaron, another Canadian, a soldier turned cook, whom the officers from Fort Russell brought with them. He never washes his face or hands, which are always black with smoke. Nor is he ever on time, especially with breakfast; true, he blames the officers; "Those gentlemen are always the last ones up," he says, "and I can't do anything with them."

Fort Laramie, guarded by such poor soldiers, is a fort only in name. No entrenchment or wall surrounds it. On the side away from the river is only a kind of ditch where the excavated dirt is thrown in a heap in one of its angles in a large circular outline, as if for the foundation of a tower. Such is the only defense work raised against the Indians. Never having been attacked since the establishment of the fort, the defenses have never been kept in repair. Beyond the ditch is the cemetery where Indians and whites sleep fraternally in their last sleep; then comes the prairie, soon marked by hillocks of rounded stones. These hillocks are strewn with pines like sand dunes which someone has wanted to fix in place, but these pines are natural growths. If you climb these knolls, you enjoy a fine view of the Platte, its left bank marked by a line of·

natural ramparts of gravelly sandstone, such as I have already described on Lone Tree Creek. From the foot of these ramparts the Platte soon arrives at its confluence with the Laramie River, and from there finds its way to North Platte, the chief station on the Pacific railroad after Omaha, and where it unites with the South Platte.

If, from the banks of the North Platte, you look toward the setting sun, you perceive on the horizon a high peak, conical in form, like the volcanic domes of Auvergne; that is Laramie Peak, isolated in the midst of the plains, serving as a point of reference for the emigrants and nomadic Indians who cross this country. This peak is aligned with the direction of the Colorado Rocky Mountains, and forms a pro-longation as a last peak toward the north. It is some 1,200 metres [about 4,000 feet] above the level of the neighboring terrain, and can be seen from very far, more than eighty miles. The prairie air is so pure, so dry and transparent, that the view of the peak is still clear at that great distance. It lifts its blue mass proudly above the horizontal plane, and the eye dwells with pleasure on its massive rocks, the only ones to be seen in ranging over the country. Farther south come the Black Hills, rich in resinous woods, pines, cedars, and firs, and streaked with rich metal-bearing lodes, it is said.[1] Still farther south, in Colorado Territory, serving as landmarks for the whole meridian, are the famous Longs Peak and Pikes Peak, which you know are the highest points of the Rocky Mountains, carrying their steep and snowy summits to the height of 5,000 metres,[2] and hailed as landmarks by all emigrants of the prairies.

The road leading from Fort Laramie to Laramie Peak was not long ago much frequented. This was the way the neophyte Mormons passed on their way to Utah, their capital on the Salt Lake; by it, too, came the emigrants who pushed on to California by land, on foot, or by wagon. It was also at one time the route chosen by the famous Overland stage. Today the gold fever has died down, at least in Eldorado, and few emigrants are so poor as to go to California by the plains route. The Mormons have seen their coffers filled and their recruits take the Pacific

[1] Not the Black Hills of South Dakota and Wyoming, but the present Laramie Hills, or Sherman Hills, west of Cheyenne and Wheatland. The reports of mineral wealth did not prove to be justified.

[2] Again Simonin's estimate is too high. See above, p. 61, footnotes 4 and 5.

railroad; even the Overland stage has had to replace its stations and moves them every day before the astonishing progress of civilization in the Far West. The iron path causes the stage to lose ground day by day. In three years the Overland Mail will no longer exist, and a double ribbon of iron will unite the two oceans, Atlantic and Pacific. Fort Laramie was the first stopping place in this unceasing march of progress. The discovery of gold mines in the Rocky Mountains and the rapid exploitation of the territory of Colorado shifted the whole plains movement southward. The only reminder of civilization in the desert at Fort Laramie is the electric telegraph.

CHAPTER 13

A Sioux Village

Fort Laramie, Dakota, 12 November

Three miles west of Fort Laramie the Sioux have installed a camp. Other children of the prairie have gathered around the fort, and with the former make up what is called the band of "Laramie Loafers," the vagrants of Laramie, so called because they live on alms, the assistance the government gives them.

The Sioux village is at the right of the road leading to Laramie Peak, and close to the river. It includes some hundred huts, or "lodges," such as may also be properly called "wigwams." It is estimated that each lodge may hold five or six individuals, more or less, an observation worth noting, because ordinarily population figures for a tribe are given in lodges.

The Indian lodge is built with a certain number of slender poles, first laid out on the ground around a common center, like the radii of a single circle, and then lifted and held inclined; in this manner all the poles are entangled one with another and mutually sustain each other at the top, where they are further bound by a cord. The opposite ends, each diverging from its neighbor, touch the ground. The conical circumference of the lodge is then covered with hides of the bison or with pieces of canvas sewed together. The top remains open. A low, narrow entrance on the side, through which one passes only by crouching, forms the door. A beaver skin or a piece of canvas, held by a nail or a hinge or sewn on above, falls down over this opening and is usually kept closed. In the center of the lodge is a fire always lighted, and on or about the fire are the pots and kettles for the meals. Often the pothook which holds the kettle hangs from the very top of the lodge. Only the opening above allows the smoke to escape or the light to enter; which is to say that for one not accustomed to it, it is impossible to stay in the lodge.

In the interior, around the circumference, are the beds, bison robes piled up to serve as covering and mattress, and apparel of all sorts such as make up their clothing, then the trunks and leather boxes in which they lock up their precious objects. In one corner are their cooking utensils, when they have any. Here and there hangs a quarter of raw bison, dried in the sun or smoked, or even with the meat drawn into strips. An indescribable disorder is everywhere, yet it appears that the Indian finds his way, and each inhabitant of the lodge has his place irrevocably assigned.

An old trader who has lived among the Sioux for many years (even has married a wife from the tribe), Père Richard,[1] was one of the first to receive me into his lodge, for he had just arrived to set up his lodge near the Laramie Loafers. At the sight of this smoke-tanned man with graying hair falling abundantly about his shoulders, I asked without too much reflection, "Are you Sioux?"

"I am French," he answered with the most tranquil air in the world and with the best of accents.

"What! You are French and live in a lodge like the savages!"

"I prefer it, it is more convenient."

That was his only reply. He presented his wife and daughter, who came timidly to give me their hand, then we smoked the peace pipe together and spoke of Paris, to which he had long contemplated a voyage. Paris is the first city the stranger always speaks of, dreaming only of savoring its pleasures. Père Richard had a further motive in wanting to see the great capital. His family had emigrated to America after the first Revolution, and he felt drawn to France as to the land of his fathers.

[1] Pierre, or Peter, Richard was established in the Fort Laramie area as early as 1846. In that year Francis Parkman described him as "a little, swarthy, black-eyed Frenchman," with a frock of smoked deerskin, gaily ornamented with porcupine quills, and "leggins" with long fringes down their sides. See Francis Parkman, *The Oregon Trail* (8th ed.; Boston: Little, Brown, 1911), p. 93.

A Sioux Village

The Sioux village, where I had scarcely expected to find a compatriot, had further curiosities to offer. Little children, boys and small girls, ran half naked about the lodges. They amused themselves by building little lodges or playing at pony, that is, they loaded one of their group with two long, dragging sticks, right and left, then placed across these sticks what pretended to represent their domestic belongings, clothing, buffalo skins, kitchen utensils, such as the Indians take with them when they move by loading their ponies or horses in this manner. Children of Redskins, children of civilized peoples, their games are ever the same: imitation of what the child sees. At home the doll which recalls the fine lady, or the household, the wooden horse, the theatre, the cardboard houses; here the pony and the little lodge.

Dogs are numerous around these lodges. The Indians own battalions of these animals, which serve them at once as defender, vigilant sentinel, and a means of nourishment.

As I went about the Sioux camp, these alert guardians, indifferent to the fate awaiting them, barked at my presence; but I calmed them with my voice and pursued my explorations. I entered many of the lodges. Here the warriors played cards in a circle, with lead balls serving as stakes. All the players maintained silence and allowed no emotion to show at gain or loss. Even less did they deign to throw a glance at their visitor. Others were playing the "game of hands," a kind of Italian *morra*,[2] and arrows stuck in the earth marked the points. Here the players accompanied themselves by a discordant chanting and the deafening music of beating together pans and tambourines.

I could not enter all the lodges. Some were severely guarded and the profane turned away. This was where they made "great medicine," or where the medicine men submitted their sick to the test of vapor baths.

Women seated in a circle labored around some lodges at needlework, adorning collars or moccasins with beads or tracing designs on a buffalo hide. They moved slowly, calculating, reflecting, counting the lines and points and being careful not to make a mistake. The old matrons prepared hides stretched on pegs. With a pebble of siliceous sandstone they scraped the hide, taking out all the blisters, then polished it with a

[2] *Morra* is an Italian finger-guessing game.

kind of steel chisel attached to the end of a bone. Formerly the edge of a stone axe, or flint or diorite (greenstone), served for this work, before iron was brought to the savage by civilized man. After being thus prepared, the buffalo skin is tanned with the brain of the same animal.

The women are far from beautiful. If most of the Indians are a proud and noble type, the "squaws" show nothing in their figures to reveal the woman as civilized nations understand the word. Timid, shamefaced, they lower their eyes before the white and hide themselves. Fatigue and hard work have altered their features. All the domestic cares fall on them. They clean the dwellings; curry the horses; prepare the meals; rear the children, or "papooses"; raise the lodges; and on the road carry all the furnishings of the lodges. The man follows on horseback, carrying only his bow and arrows. To top it off, the women are often beaten. They are regarded as slaves by their husbands, who marry as many women as they wish. Parents willingly give their consent for a horse, for a few buffalo hides, and all is done. Chastity is not strictly enforced, but often the husband cuts off the nose or the ears of an unfaithful wife. Among the Redskins each is his own judge and applies the law in his own fashion.

Sometimes the wife is sold when the husband becomes displeased with her. White women taken prisoners by the Indians and installed in their lodges are no better treated. However, they are respected in some tribes, and it must be assumed that in this case it is the white skin which is distasteful to the Redskin. It is clear now why the Indian male, always on horseback, in war or in the hunt, is good-looking and well built, and why the squaws, submitted to so many burdens, are, contrary to the usual expectation, in their own setting the uglier half of the human race. It is only fair to say that in the Sioux villages not all the women fit equally into this description; a few are even pretty and approach the white type. It is easy to see that they are of mixed blood.

The Laramie Loafers are not the only band camped here. The Crows recently arrived, advised over a month ago that the commission would be at Fort Laramie around the tenth of November, at the time of the full moon. To respond to the invitation of the commissioners, they left the extreme north of Dakota, the borders of the Yellowstone where they were hunting at the time.[3] Some twenty of their chiefs, with their wives, their children, and their braves (the lieutenants of the chiefs), have made the journey despite the snow and the distance, and despite the Sioux, with whom they are at war. These latter could have stopped them on the way, for they had to cross enemy territory to reach the rendezvous.

As men who know their own worth, the Crows have camped at a certain distance from the Indian "loafers," though their tents, being of the same kind, might easily be confused. The men differ in type, however, for the Crows are surely the proudest of the prairie Indians, at least of the northern Indians. Their features are wide in proportions, broadly accented, their stature gigantic, their form athletic. Their majestic faces recall the types of the Roman Caesars, as they are engraved on medallions.

I entered the lodge of the chief. "Shake hands with each," said an officer who had already been within the tent; "they are all great chiefs." I obeyed his advice and touched in turn the hand of the sixteen sachems seated in a circle, each time making the gutteral sound "A'hou!" which serves as a greeting among the Redskins. Each in turn repeated my salute, and some clasped my hand hard enough to crack the bones. This lively evidence of friendliness among Indians ordinarily so impassive surprised me. No doubt these brave fellows thought they were dealing with some influential member of the commission, from whom they expected special concessions and exceptional gifts. The ceremony of greeting completed, we smoked the calumet. Each Crow drew some puffs on the pipe and passed it in the same way to his neighbor. No one spoke.

I profited by the silence to examine these men at leisure. I have already mentioned their athletic form. Their faces and cheeks were tattooed with red vermillion. They were scantily clothed, here one with a woolen blanket, there one with a buffalo skin or a part of an officer's uniform; another had a quite naked torso. A number wore necklaces or earrings of shells or of animal teeth. One had around his neck a silver medal with the likeness of a president of the United States (Pierce),

[3] Dakota Territory at this time included parts of the present states of Wyoming and Montana.

a gift to him in Washington when he was there on a mission in 1853. Another wore on his chest a rather crudely worked silver horse, and from this ornament got the name of White Horse, by which he was known. A wounded old chief lay in the corner of the lodge, his leg pierced by two bullets and held in a cast installed by the Indians themselves. He returned my salute with a sad glance, pointing to the sick member which prevented him from rising.

The Crows are not the only nomadic Indians I have met at Laramie. Two Arapaho chiefs from La Porte (the frontier of Colorado), representing the tattooed ones of the North (Arapaho signifies the tattooed ones in Indian, I am told), are camped on a small island in the middle of the river. They have come to Laramie to take part in the conference at the same time as the Crows, from whom they differ sharply by their haggard and somber type.

The different tribes of the North, especially those which in the aggregate compose the great nation of the Sioux, were among those most impatiently awaiting the commissioners; but the Crows alone came. Mr. Beauvais, the principal agent of the commission, several months ago dispatched from Saint Louis to Fort Laramie, had promised to bring in the Sioux, but the Sioux have not come. They are at the moment hunting very far away, and do not wish to be disturbed. Express messenger after express messenger has been sent to them, to whom some have replied that it was too cold to undertake so long a voyage, others that the whites have always deceived them and they no longer wish to come at their call. Some of them, showing themselves insolent, have consigned the United States commission to all the devils. "Let the Great Father (the President of the United States) recall his young men (soldiers) from our country," the chief of the band of Bad Faces, Red Cloud, answered the messenger of the commission; "then we shall sign a treaty that will last forever."[4] All the chiefs present, especially the warrior Big Ribs, loudly applauded these words of Red Cloud.

The Cheyennes of the North showed themselves neither more polite nor more inclined to hurry than the Sioux. Poor Mr. Beauvais, whom the Indians call Gros Ventre because of his corpulence, can do no more,

[4] Red Cloud had sent word that he would not confer with the peace commissioners unless U.S. troops were withdrawn from the Bozeman Trail.

though he would willingly go on foot to the Sioux, even to Red Cloud's band, to bring them in by sheer force.

Tired of waiting, the commission has decided that it will open the council with the Crows tomorrow morning at ten o'clock, and will confer also with the Arapahos who came from La Porte. In the meantime it has received official depositions from certain traders from Montana Territory. These have reported the devastations committed by the Indians of that region, but recently settled by Americans who are exploiting the gold and silver mines. The deponents have not failed to report also the complaints of the Indians against the whites.

The governor of Colorado, the honorable Mr. Hunt,[5] was also heard, and gave the commissioners an account of the recent pillaging by Cheyennes and Arapahos.

Such are the preliminaries by which the commission of the United States prepares for the great conference, or "powwow," to be opened with the savages, carrying out strictly its mandate and weighting the scale in favor of neither white nor Redskin.

[5] Alexander C. Hunt served as governor of Colorado Territory from 1867 to 1869.

CHAPTER 14

Mountain Men, Trappers, and Traders

Fort Laramie, Dakota, 13 November

At the news of our arrival, all the hunters of the Great West came hastening to Fort Laramie, buffalo hunters and beaver trappers, traders who do business with the tribes, all those energetic adventurers of the Rocky Mountains whom the Americans designate by the term "mountain men." They knew the commission was coming and arrived ahead of time. I saw here Père Bisonette, an old Louisianian of French origin. He lives now on a farm at Fort Laramie. He has always frequented these latitudes, for Fort Laramie, before being a military post was, as I have written, a trading post belonging to the celebrated firm of Chouteau of St. Louis. If you have read Fremont's account of his expedition to the Far West, you will have noted that when Fremont stopped at Fort Laramie he made mention of Bisonette.[1]

"He has earned money as thick as your arm," said Pallardy to me. "Beauvais and I were his agents, we worked under him. Today it is we who are rich and he is poor. What do you expect? We gamble and amuse ourselves to pass the time in the desert. Women, good cheer, they will take you far! Bisonette has lost everything, but he is still a good fellow."

[1] Joseph Bisonette had acted briefly as interpreter and guide west on the North Platte for John Charles Fremont in 1842, but turned back in a few days. In 1846 Francis Parkman mentioned Bisonette as a trader at the head of Horse Creek. See John Charles Fremont, *Memoirs of My Life* (Chicago: Bedford, Clarke and Co., 1887), I, 115–123, 159, *passim*.

96

Another trader of pure French origin (he came from Havre) invited us today to his tent for a meal of dog; we have to say it without mincing words. We ate a young dog, fattened and killed for our benefit. The flesh of the finest sheep could not compare with it, and I understand the custom of the Redskin of reserving the dog for holiday feasts, especially when they wish to honor the whites.

"How do you find this meat?" asked General Harney, who has grown old amid Indian wars, and who perhaps for the hundredth time was sitting down to such a meal.

"Excellent, General."

"Have you eaten horse meat in Paris? For I have heard that you have become eaters of horse meat."

"Not yet; but when I return I shall certainly taste horse meat, if only to compare it with dog."

The truth is, I have never eaten better mutton than this young dog at Fort Laramie.

Our host was called Guerut. He left Havre twenty years ago to make his fortune in the United States (one always comes to this country to make his fortune), and has finally, after many vicissitudes, lost himself at the end of the Far West. Today he is an interpreter for the Laramie Loafers at the fort.

Among the traders to come to Laramie is also Père Richard, whom I have already mentioned. I go from time to time to smoke the peace pipe, the true calumet of the Redskins, with him.

"I have earned lots of money with the Sioux," he told me recently, "but one day the Cheyennes, those good-for-nothing savages, took me prisoner while they were at war with my friends, the Sioux. They stole all my horses, all my fine buffalo robes, all the beaver skins I had prepared. I still have a few dollars left, and I am not completely poor. I want to go this winter into the Black Hills[2] to cut ties for the railroad. You can earn a few dollars there. I know forests of cedar and pine which belong to no one; I'll make something by selling them."

Among all these rovers of the Great Plains, these old trappers, all of whom recall France to me, whether the old France of Canada or

[2] Again, the present Laramie Hills, or Sherman Hills, rather than the Black Hills of South Dakota and Wyoming.

Louisiana or modern France, the best type is still our guide and interpreter, Pallardy. And yet what a lot he still does not know about the savages. I tried to question him on the origins, the legends, the traditions of the Redskins among whom he has so long lived. One evening around the campfire, during the last days of our trip from Hillsdale to Fort Laramie, thinking that the Canadian would be communicative, I asked him if the Sioux whom he knew so well, and whose language he spoke, had not preserved some tradition of their first coming to America.

"I have never bothered my head about that," Pallardy answered. "Ask me the price of buffalo hides or beaver skins, I can tell you about that. But legends, origins, as you call them, that doesn't interest me."

And I could get no more from him. Of the Sioux language I learned a little more. Thanks to him, I am able to count in the Sioux language, at once guttural and harmonious, reminding one much of the Spanish when it is spoken. I have drawn up a little dictionary of the common words in Sioux, which I shall show you in Paris.

Pallardy has also initiated me into the language of signs, which all the Redskins use among themselves to communicate from one tribe to another, and which has many analogies with the language of our deaf mutes.

As to the Crows and the Arapahos, no one could give me lessons in their languages. They are more guttural and, at least the Arapaho, pronounced only at the front of the lips. No interpreter is able to write them, and even when he understands them, can often speak with them only by signs. The thickest Arab speech is nothing beside these diabolical languages.

Linguists, anthropologists, ethnologists, should be able to tell us why these tribes, neighboring on each other, have languages so dissimilar and present such different physical types. The problem raises plenty of difficulties for the partisans of the unity of the human race, but this is not the place to solve it—I merely mention it in passing.

Instead, I shall conclude with a last word on these vigorous trappers, these bold traders, who so courageously pursue their habits of hunting, trade, and travel on the prairies, among the Indian tribes, habits first introduced by France and not forgotten by her children. These rovers of the plains are pioneers in their fashion, and, after having lived briefly in their midst, sharing their tents and their meals, I should be ashamed if I had not devoted a few lines to them. Honor to these distant children of old France! I am sure you already admire them as I do.

CHAPTER 15

The Great Council of the Crows

Fort Laramie, Dakota, 14 November

Shall I describe in detail the council of the Redskins with the peace commissioners?[1] It might be of interest. It will help me to pass the time, and what better to do in this fort?

You recall that day before yesterday the great chiefs of the Crows were convoked in solemn conference by the commissioners of the Union. The sun rose radiant that day, the sky was cloudless, the weather of an exceptional mildness. Comparing the temperature with that of the previous days, when they had suffered so greatly, coming on horseback from the ends of Dakota, the old sachems must have thought the Great Spirit was finally showing himself to be favorable. If the sun, one of their divinities, consented to smile, doubtless they would profit in their cause in the great powwow with the whites.

The hour set for the opening of the palaver was ten in the morning. The Indians, who never hurry and who tell time only by the sun, were a little late; perhaps they were concluding their big medicine ceremonies. Finally they appeared, adorned in their finest costumes. Some were on horseback. These forded the Laramie River, while others came by the bridge, followed by their women and children, squaws and papooses. The wife of Bear Tooth, one of the chief orators, was on

---

[1] The Peace Commission, in its official report of January 7, 1868, allotted but two brief paragraphs to the Fort Laramie council. See 40 Cong., 2d Sess., *House Exec. Doc. 97*, p. 5.

horseback like her husband, whom she never left. Indian women ride straddle like the men.

The great chief Black Foot, having dismounted, made a sign for his braves or warriors to line up. Each had on a different costume, one a buffalo skin over a linen shirt, another, a woolen blanket and a jacket of deer skin, ornamented with fringes but missing its decoration of scalps, which the Indians hardly dare exhibit before the whites. Scalps were left at home that day. Another wore an officer's coat and pantaloons without any seat; fortunately, the tails of the coat were sufficiently long.

Several had the head covered with a hat of black felt, Calabrian style, like those of American generals. The whole hat, to its full height, was ornamented about with a series of multicolored ribbons. Some chiefs wore leggings and leather moccasins. All had ears and neck loaded with necklaces and earrings of shells or animal teeth. Not satisfied with all these ornaments, one Crow had added to his hair an imitation hair like a tail reaching from the crown to the sole of his feet. This queue was not variegated like that of the great chief of the Brulés, but strewn with silver discs, round, not too thick, made by the patient beating out of American dollars or other pieces of less value. The discs diminished in size regularly from head to feet, and the pride with which the sachem bore this finery would lead one to surmise that he would not part with it for an empire. The Indians must attach great value to this ornament, otherwise costly, for it is found among all tribes.

The chief with the long headdress was not the only one to attract attention. One Crow wore with pride a large medallion which he had recently received in Washington from the hands of the President. Another, lacking this official medallion, made use of a Mexican dollar. In turn, White Horse had not forgotten to decorate himself with the silver horse which gives him his name, and which hangs like a medal on his chest. With it goes a square bag of gray canvas, far from clean, in which he has carefully enclosed his mirror. Like most Redskins, he is very much concerned with his attire and the figure he makes.

Beside him march Lodge Pole Tip, Man Who Was Shot in the Face, and Bird in the Nest, three chiefs or warriors of great reputation among

101

the Crows. Most of their faces are tattooed in red vermillion and in yellow or blue. In the midst of the group may be seen the poor wounded man mentioned above, his leg stiff in the dressing which holds it. The old chief wanted to come at all hazards; he was hoisted onto his horse and helped down with great difficulty, and followed as best he could, hobbling along.

After being lined up, the sachems intoned a song of their nation, solemn and somber, mingled with discordant cries and sometimes sharp yelpings. The basses, baritones, and tenors observed no tempo in this chorus, and yet this primitive, savage music goes well with the type of singers and the setting.

In this way the chiefs advanced in single file, slowly, in perfect order, ignoring the crowd which pressed about them. Never had the athletic form and majestic figure of the Crows appeared more dignified. Then they broke rank and entered the room of the interpreters. There they were soon advised that the commission awaited them to open the conference.

The hall where the powwow was held is of considerable dimensions. It is built of wood, and can easily hold 250 to 500 persons; it formerly served as a storehouse for the quartermaster of the fort.

The Crow chiefs, seated together on benches, each in the place assigned him by his rank, the commissioners each in his single seat, formed a circle such that one might say that extreme civilization faced extreme barbarism. The orator's place would be in the center of the circle. On one side were the interpreters and the Indian agents; on the other, the clerk, the secretary of the commission, the newspaper reporters, etc. Women and children of the chiefs were there; and a few women, the oldest matrons among them, sat on the benches with the chiefs, among them Running Water, Yellow Mare, and Woman Who Killed a Bear. The papooses, some even at the breast, often disturbed the peace of the assembly with their cries and tears, but no one paid them any attention, especially the Crows.

The Laramie Loafers, the three great chiefs of the Sioux, guided by Pallardy, officers, soldiers, and employees of the fort, everyone, had come to witness the debates about to open. The commission, in its paternal and generous way, had closed the door to no one.

The Great Council of the Crows

When silence was established, Dr. Matthews,[2] United States agent for the Crows, arose and said in English: "I have the honor to present to the peace commission the chiefs of the Crow nation," and turning toward the chiefs, he said in Crow: "Here are the commissioners sent from Washington to make peace with you, and you will see if I have told you lies."

The interpreter for the Crows, Pierre Chêne, a Canadian of both Irish and French blood, translated these words into English for the commission. He is aided in his duties by John Richard, half Sioux, son of that Frenchman, Père Richard, who had temporarily set up his tent with all his family in the midst of the Laramie Loafers, and whom you now know as well as I.

Pierre Chêne and Richard do not shine as interpreters. They translate the eloquent speeches of the day into bad English, without regard for the genius of the Crow language, and they make the commissioners regret the worthy spokesmen whom they have just left at the council with the five nations of the South.[3]

The presentation of the Crows to the commission, and the latter to the Crows, falls within the American custom, which stems from the English. In the United States one should be introduced to another before speaking to him.

While these double introductions were taking place, the Crows were heard to give their low cry, "A'hou!" which serves at once for the prairie Indian's salute and his sign of approval. At the same time, the calumet circled from mouth to mouth, while the sachems, silent, immovable, appeared to be quite indifferent.

Finally, Bear Tooth arose, took three puffs on the peace pipe, and presented it to Dr. Matthews, saying: "Smoke, and remember me today and grant what I ask"; then, passing it to General Harney, he said:

[2] Washington Matthews, a medical doctor, had been stationed in Dakota Territory as an army surgeon. He had studied Indian languages intensively.

[3] This council, held in Kansas in October on the Medicine Lodge Creek, a tributary of the Arkansas, was concluded by a solemn treaty of peace signed by the Comanches, Apaches, Kiowas, Cheyennes, and Arapahos. All consented to withdraw to the reservations indicated by the commissioners, on the borders of the Red River in the south of Indian Territory, where for many years the Cherokees, the Creeks, the Choctaws, the Osages, and other tribes from the Atlantic states had already accepted reservations. [*Simonin's note.*] See above, p. 60, footnote 2.

"Smoke, father, and have pity on me"; and to President Taylor: "Father, smoke, and remember me and my people, for we are poor"; and again, offering the peace pipe to Generals Augur, Terry, Sanborn, and Colonel Tappan, "And you also, father." Each of the commissioners, putting the pipe to his lips, took a puff and returned it to Bear Tooth, inclining his head as a token of assent, or giving the guttural cry of "A'hou!" This done, Bear Tooth sat down and said that he was ready, he and his nation, to listen to the words of the whites. Then, amid profound silence, President Taylor arose and read the following speech, each phrase of which was translated into Crow by the interpreter Chêne. I reproduce it here for you literally in French:

"My friends, chiefs, captains, and warriors of the Crow nation, the Great Spirit made all men and that is why we are brothers. On our invitation, you have made a long journey with the greatest difficulties to come to see us. We too have traveled a long distance to see you and to shake your hand. Your Great Father in Washington, even though he is far away from you, is informed of your good will. He knows your friendship for his white children. He knows, too, how many proofs of peace you have given the government. He knows the troubles that besiege you. He has sent us to see and to learn from your mouths your condition. We shall thus be able to advise the necessary measures to drive all trouble from you, and to travel a good path together. We learn that rich mines have been found in your country, and that the whites in some cases have taken possession of them. We learn also that some roads have been opened across your territory, that settlements have been established, that the buffalo which you hunt have been scattered afar and even rapidly diminish. We know finally that the whites become more and more numerous around you, and take possession of your best lands to occupy them permanently.

"It is because such things have taken place that we are sent to you by your Great Father of Washington. We are sent to take measures which will mend this shameful situation as much as possible, and at the same time will protect you against all future inconvenience. We wish to set aside a part of your territory for your nation, where you may live forever, you and your children, and where your Great Father in Washington will permit no white to settle. We wish you to indicate the section of your territory which will suit you best for this purpose. And when you have thus marked out this territory, which we can never occupy, we wish to buy from you the rest of your lands for our use, leaving you for all time the right to hunt there as long as the buffalo remain there. In the reserved land which you will choose, we intend to build a house for your agent, a mill to saw your wood, a mill to grind your grain, a forge, a house for your farmer, and all the other houses that may be necessary. We wish also on these reserved lands to furnish the horses and animals which will assure you of provisions and sustain your families when the buffalo have disappeared. We wish also to send you warm clothing each year, to cover you comfortably, and those tools of agriculture which will make you capable of earning your own living by working the land. So that your children may become as intelligent as the whites, we wish to send you teachers who will instruct them. You have made our hearts happy by coming here to see us, and you will not go away with empty hands. We have presents for you on the way. They must already be here. We shall always be grateful to you for the peaceful sentiments you have never ceased to show toward our people, and we expect in the future to show you our full friendship by our acts. Now, we wish to hear from you all that you have to say to us. We shall give all our attention to your words, and we shall answer you in the best spirit. I have spoken."

The first part of this discourse was received on the part of the Crows with marks of general approval, and interrupted by those guttural sounds which are the Indian parallel of our "Good! Very good! Bravo!" in our legislative bodies. The second part was heard, on the contrary, with defiance and amid a glacial silence.

When the president had finished, the peace pipe continued to pass from mouth to mouth, and the Indians appeared to consult together. One of the commissioners, General Sanborn, to dissipate the cloud and restore calm to the minds of the Crows, asked the interpreter to make them understand that the whites did not wish to occupy all their territory, but only that part which was already on the way to settlement. This did not seem to convince the sachems.

Nevertheless, Bear Tooth arose: "What you have said to me, I have completely understood. I have come to see you, and I shall say to

105

you what I think." Then, shaking the hand of President Taylor, he said: "Father, I have come from far to see you, do me justice"; then to General Harney: "Father, you have sent for me; listen well to me"; then to General Augur: "Father, I am happy to see you and to shake your hand; do something for me"; and to General Terry: "Father, I am very tired; I am a poor man; I have come from far to see you"; and to General Sanborn: "Father, do something for me; on my way here I have camped where wood and grass were lacking, and where it was very cold; my horses are tired"; and finally, addressing Colonel Tappan: "Father, look at me; I am poor; love me as I love you and grant me what I ask of you."

Four times Bear Tooth made the rounds of the half circle occupied by the commission, repeating the same formulas which he scarcely varied, and each time shaking the hands of the commissioners. One wondered when this preparatory appeal would end, but Dr. Matthews had taken pains to warn the assembly that it was a Crow custom to repeat the hand-shaking ceremony four times with those they wish most to honor. At the end Bear Tooth, taking a buffalo robe from the hands of his wife, who was present, presented it to General Harney, saying: "Father, you have white hairs, protect yourself with this skin; it will shelter you against the cold." Then the orator went to the center of the circle occupied on one side by the Indians, on the other by the commissioners, and asked permission to speak seated. The interpreter translated his speech sentence by sentence into English; and here is what he said, as I wrote it down myself, a stenographic report in English, so to speak, under the dictation of the interpreter:

"Fathers, last spring I was on foot on the mountain of the bighorn sheep, and one of your young men told me you were coming to visit us. My white father asked me to come a part of the way. I hesitated, for I was far, very far; but finally I agreed to start on the way. This autumn, when the leaves of the trees were falling, the Crows were on the banks of the river of the Yellowstone. Your messenger brought me ten chests of tobacco, and made known your wish that we should come to Laramie. In answer I said yes, yes. I should have preferred that my white father come to Fort Philip Kearny, and not to Laramie, and I say that if he had pushed that far, I should have answered affirmatively to all that he should have asked; but in the meantime the bad days came, and I had to come to Laramie. It was cold, and my horses looked very poor. Therefore it is my white father who will answer yes, yes, to all the requests I shall make of him.

"Fathers, I have made a long journey to come to see you. I left from Fort Smith; I am very poor; I am hungry, I am cold. We found on the way neither buffalo, nor wood, nor water. Look at me, all of you who hear me. I am a man like you. I have a head and a face like you. We are all one and the same people. I want my children and my nation to prosper and live long years."

Then, rising, Bear Tooth went toward the commissioners Taylor and Harney, and grasping their hands convulsively, he cried three times: "Fathers, fathers, fathers, hear me well. Call back your young men from the mountains of the bighorn sheep. They have run over our country; they have destroyed the growing wood and the green grass; they have set fire to our lands. Fathers, your young men have devastated the country and killed my animals, the elk, the deer, the antelope, my buffalo. They do not kill them to eat them; they leave them to rot where they fall. Fathers, if I went into your country to kill your animals, what would you say? Should I not be wrong, and would you not make war on me? Well, the Sioux have offered me hundreds of mules and horses to go to war with them, and I have not done so.

"A long time ago you made a treaty with the Crow nation; then you took with you one of our chiefs to the States. You understand well what I mean, I suppose. This chief has never returned. Where is he? We have not seen him again, and we are weary of waiting. Give us what he left. We, his friends, his relatives, we have come to know his last wishes.

"I learn that you have also sent messengers to the Sioux. You have made them, as us, presents of tobacco; but the Sioux have told me that they would not come, for you have always deceived them. The Sioux said to us: "Ah! The white fathers have sent for you, and you are going to see them. They will treat you as they have treated us. Go and see, and come back and tell us what you have heard. The white fathers will seduce your ears with fine words and soft promises which they will never keep. Go and see them, they will make sport of you!

107

"I let the Sioux talk and I came to visit you. When I return, I expect to lose half of my horses on the way.

"Fathers, fathers, I am not at all ashamed to speak before you. The Great Spirit has made us all, but he placed the red man in the center, with the whites all about. Make me an intelligent Indian. Ah! my heart overflows, it is full of bitterness. All the Crows, the old chiefs of former days, our ancestors, our grandfathers, our grandmothers, often said to us: 'Be friends with the white faces, for they are powerful!' We, their children, have obeyed, and see what has happened.

"Long ago, more than forty years ago, the Crows camped on the Missouri. Our chief was shot in the head by a white man." (Here General Harney interrupted the orator and said, "The white chief was mad, I was there, I saw it.")

"One day, on the river of the Yellowstone, three wagons were camped. There were three white men and a white woman with them. Four Crows came to them asking for a piece of bread. One of the white men took his rifle and fired. Sorrel Horse, a chief, was hit and died. We, we forget this misdeed. And I tell you these things to show you that the palefaces have done wrong as well as the Indians.

"Some time ago I went to Fort Benton, for we too have done wrong. My young men had fired by mistake on the whites. I asked the pardon of the white chief. I gave him nine mules and sixty buffalo robes in payment for the wrong we had done. It is thus I pay for our wrongs.

"From there, I went to Fort Smith, on the banks of the Bighorn, and I found whites there. I presented myself to shake hands with the officers, but they responded by putting their fists in my face and throwing me to the ground. It is thus we are treated by your young men.

"Fathers, you have spoken to me of digging in the earth and raising animals. I do not wish to listen to such speeches. I was raised with the buffalo and I love them. Since my birth, I have learned, like your chiefs, how to be strong, to take up my tent when it is necessary and to go across the prairie according to my good pleasure. Have pity on me, I am weary of speaking.

"And you, father," addressing President Taylor and giving him moccasins, "take these moccasins and keep your feet warm."

The Great Council of the Crows

Bear Tooth's speech was interrupted on the side of the Indians by frequent marks of assent, and the commissioners themselves were heard to give their approval to certain passages in no uncertain tone. The orator, uninfluenced by any sign of applause, continued his speech slowly, stopping at each sentence to let the interpreter translate, then taking up without difficulty the thread of his discourse, as if he had delivered it as a whole. Nevertheless he improvised.

The Crow language lent a further charm to the speech of Bear Tooth, a language at once harmonious and musical yet somewhat guttural, recalling, like the Sioux, the frequent vowels and aspirates of the Spanish. He accompanied his speech with mild, cadenced gestures, noble and graceful, and, still better, in harmony with the ideas he wished to express. Gestures constitute a universal language among the Redskins, like the signs of the deaf mutes.

"I understood everything the Crows said," said Swift Bear, one of the Sioux chiefs, to Pallardy, as they left the conference, "just from the gestures he made."

When Bear Tooth had finished speaking, Black Foot, another great orator of the Crows, arose and shooks hands with each of the commissioners, thanking the white fathers for coming to see the Redskins, and confirming what Bear Tooth had said, that the Crows were poor and weary; that they had suffered on the way from cold, hunger, and lack of water; and that their horses were sad to see. He begged each of the commissioners individually to hear him with patience, with an attentive ear, and to do justice to his requests.

Finally, discarding his buffalo robe, he laid it on the shoulders of President Taylor, saying, "Keep this robe, because by accepting it you recognize that you are my brother."

And then, going to the middle of the council and with his hands throwing back his long, black locks, which fell halfway to his waist, he spoke:

"When the Crows need arrows, they make them from bits of iron; when they need fire, they rub two stones against one another and light a fire to warm themselves with; when they wish to carve their meat, they make knives of stone, and these they use on the animals they kill in the hunt. All these things the Crows know very well how to do; but if they go on the reservations which the whites select for them,

109

they will not know how to drive the oxen or how to work the earth with the plow. That is why they do not wish to hear these things spoken of. Let the white fathers instead give them horses to hunt the buffalo with and rifles to kill them, and all will be well. The Great Spirit has made man and woman to live together, the man to hunt and the woman to work. We do not wish to change anything in this state of affairs.

"Fathers, I have always been a friend of the whites, and I wish to continue to be so. I was brought up as a savage, but I have never done wrong to anyone. Several years ago, the whites came to the Crows to buy the path to California, which passes by Fort Laramie. For this path they agreed to pay fifty years of indemnities. The Crows received these indemnities for two or three years only. It was after we signed this treaty that one of our great chiefs went to your country. We have never seen him since. We wish to know what happened to him, if he went up into the clouds or if he went under the earth. . . ."

Black Foot then recounted the past history of his nation. Then it was powerful, today it is poor; it was as if the Great Spirit had withdrawn from them. "What use to make treaties, if this is the way the whites observe them?"

"Do not speak to us of confining us to one corner of our territory; give up first of all the route to Powder River.[4] Recall your young men who have camped all along this path and all those who seek for gold. They are the cause of all our wars and all our misfortunes." Here the orator's voice wavered, his body trembled, the perspiration ran in large drops on his face, and his eyes shone with an unusual gleam. So must the old prophets of Israel have appeared before the kings of Asia, when they came to make known the complaints of the Jewish people.

Pausing for a moment, Black Foot once more threw back his long locks; then, passing his hand over his forehead as if to collect his memory, he recalled, like Bear Tooth, amid the low murmurs of approval from the Indians, all the bad treatment of the whites toward the Crows, who had done no wrong. He pointed out the frauds of the agents who had sold them damaged flour, from which five or six Indians once died, or who gave them useless merchandise for good buffalo robes. Then, rising to his full height and proudly raising his arm, he cried:

4 I.e., the Bozeman Trail.

The Great Council of the Crows

"But in all this my heart is of rock; I do not wish to complain." Then recalling how they had been fraudulently deprived of their lands: "Though I am poor, I shall not die, my arm is firm, and I can still hunt the buffalo as my fathers hunted it. . . . Your young men are mad, call them back. They are like children; they do not know what they need; they kill the buffalo just for pleasure and to amuse themselves, while we suffer from hunger and become poor. If you want peace, send your soldiers back to the East; let them live there, but not among us, where they bring trouble and war." And then, striking both hands against his broad, naked chest: "My grandfathers advised the nation of the Crows to be good. How can we be good, when you take our lands, promising in return so many things which you never give us? We are not slaves, and we are not dogs. One day, at Fort Smith, when I asked some food from the soldiers, they struck me on the head with a club. When I remember that, I become bad and wild. Are there no men in your country, that you send us these well-clothed children to put these vexations on us?" And his lip curled in contempt, and he stretched toward one of the commissioners a hand seized with a convulsive trembling.

"We want to live as we have been raised, hunting the animals of the prairie. Do not speak to us of shutting us up on reservations and making us cultivate the land. Let us follow the buffalo. Send your farmers, but so long as they are not for us. The Crow moves his camp across the plains and hunts the buffalo and the antelope. That is what he loves. Fathers, look at me and look at all the Crows; they all hold the same thoughts as I do. If you give us a white man for agent and trader, I wish it to be John Richard, Pierre Chêne, and Doctor Matthews. They are honest and do not lie" (agreement from all the Crows). "Look at me, and look at my people. I am not ashamed to speak to you." And then, going again to shake the hand of the commissioners, he said to each in a milder voice, "Father, do something for me; I am tired and I have spoken long." And he took his seat in silence and took the calumet which was passed to him, his head lowered and his face thoughtful.

When Black Foot had resumed his seat, an old Crow arose who from the opening of the council had held in his hand a long rod which he had brought with him that morning. This third orator, named the Wolf, is

111

also the learned one of the band, friend of fables, which he tells at need. After proceeding according to the custom with the ceremony of shaking hands, he took his place in the center of the half circle, all the time holding his long rod in his hand. It was of hard hickory wood, with six knobs on it. The Wolf called each one of these knobs a generation of men, and demonstrated how each generation is born, develops and dies, giving place to another one. Each one of these generations was then compared by the Wolf to a generation of the Crows. His nation had been friends of the whites during all that space of time. "So that the present shall continue the same," cried the orator then, whose end to his fable was impatiently awaited by the commissioners, "send no more wagons on the route to the Powder River, especially send no more soldiers. Recall your young men from our country, and then we shall be happy and will live in harmony with you, as we have lived in the generations before."

This speech, as humorous as the others had been serious, proves to the commissioners that the principle of mingling the agreeable with the useful is in favor even among the Indians. But the hour is now advanced. It is one hour after noon; they have been in conference for more than three hours. The clerk, the reporters, the commissioners can take no more. As for the Indians, smoking the peace pipe all the time, they remain impassive on their benches, and certainly would remain there until evening if they were not dismissed. Nevertheless, it is time to break up the meeting, which President Taylor does, adjourning the council until the next morning.

The chiefs withdrew slowly, one by one, followed by their squaws. Each came to shake the hand of the commissioners. The old men and the matrons even embraced the president and General Harney, by rubbing their cheeks and their noses on those of the whites, leaving not a little vermillion on the white skins. The Americans are not bothered by so small a matter, and accept the embrace of the Redskins with as good grace as they did the ceremony of hand shaking and smoking the peace pipe.

The orators and their band did not return to their tent without eating. On leaving the council, they went to the interpreters' quarters and there shared in the meal offered by the commissioners, though the latter dined elsewhere. Without knives or forks, seated on the floor or on the cots, the Indians seized upon great quarters of beef or of roast mutton. When they had bitten off whole mouthfuls, they passed the meat on fraternally to the next one. Their drink was black coffee, which circulated in enormous earthenware cups. These were frequently refilled from a vast kettle, which gave off a pleasant steam in the middle of the quarters. The Crows did full honor to every dish, but the banquet was calm and silent, and no one disputed with his neighbor for a place or for a choice morsel. During the meal some Sioux women from the camp of the Laramie Loafers came out of curiosity and seated themselves in front of the door of the feast hall. To pass the time, they rendered the same service to each other as the peasant women of Naples do, searching through each others' hair; but the feasters paid no attention to them and continued their eating.

In the evening there was dancing in the open air in front of Père Richard's tent. There again coffee circulated freely. A fire had been lighted in the midst of the circle of the dancers, who began their war dance and singing, followed by the women. The movements were at first very slow, then, finally, violent. Their legs particularly are always in motion, and the men give off howls in cadence. All this is frightening when it is a prelude to some combat, or when they dance around a prisoner whom they will put to death after torture. But in front of old Richard's tent, the Crow dance did not show its more sinister character; indeed, it soon wearied the spectators, who were bored by these monotonous movements and songs, which, nevertheless, do indicate a further resemblance between the Redskins and the Asiatic races from which it is argued that they come. The red peoples do not have, like the blacks, the gift of dance and song. Even the Crows finally wearied of their music and their cadenced steps. At an early hour they went to their sleep and to prepare for the morrow's council.

Today, at the indicated hour of ten, the Crows did not appear. The deliberations of the previous day had not been wholly friendly, and we wondered if the Indians would return to the council. They finally appeared, but singly and not in compact order as before. Bear Tooth was absent; he sent word that he was ill and that he felt the need to return home and to eat fresh buffalo. The truth was that there had been a dispute the previous evening between the Arapahos and the Crows. The latter were supposed to share with their red brothers a beef given them by the commission, and consented with bad grace. Nevertheless, Bear Tooth soon showed up, as always, accompanied by his wife, and came and took his place in the council, which had already begun.

This time all took place without the ceremonies of the preceding day; the introductions had been made, and it was in some manner a continuation of the previous meeting.

President Taylor opened the council by replying to the speeches of the Crows. Following his custom,' he read his speech, and he read it coldly, with great deliberation. The official speeches were throughout the same, prepared and read without animation or life. Mr. Taylor would have done better to improvise some warm words before these chiefs whose speeches of the preceding day had been such models of eloquence and had indicated in some degree the methods which the white orators should always follow in their powwows with the Indians.

The president thanked the Crows for not having avenged themselves against those who had mistreated them, and said he would inform the Great Father of their good behavior and of the misdeeds of the whites, who would be punished. "In the future," he said, "tell your agent immediately, and he will see that you receive justice. . . . You will not go away this time with empty hands, and we shall replace the horses which you have lost. . . . The chief whom you sent to the United States was well treated and received presents. We have followed him on his return as far as the Missouri. There he disappeared suddenly, whether he was assassinated or drowned in the river by falling from the steamer. We are greatly grieved by this accident, and we propose to give two horses to the family of this chief as compensation." Here the interpreter remarked that two of the family were present, White Horse and another old sachem, who showed great pleasure at this unexpected present.

"You say," continued the president, "that you prefer to live as you have always lived, instead of being shut up on reservations. It is for your good that we select these reservations; the buffalo are rapidly growing less, and in a few years will be entirely gone. . . . The whites are now on the Great Plains, and have built towns even to the shores

114

of the western sea. . . . We wish, while there is still time, to guarantee to you a territory which shall forever be yours and your children's. You will not need to go to it at once. Hunt now where you please, but on this territory which will be reserved for you, no white may set foot; the Great Father will drive them off with rifle shots." Marks of enthusiasm and approval. White Horse rose and went to shake hands with the commissioners.

"Next spring we shall make a decision on the subject of abandoning the road to Powder River. The season is now too advanced for us to leave the forts which we have along this route. . . .[5] If the Sioux cease to make war on us, it is possible that we shall re-cede this part of your territory to you. . . . You have asked for Pierre Chêne and John Richard as traders, and for Dr. Matthews as agent. We consent to give them to you. . . . Remember well what I have told you as coming from all the commissioners. Make it known when you have returned to your homes, and keep the memory of it in mind. I have spoken."

This speech ended, the president asked if any of the chiefs present had any remarks to make. Black Foot arose and said that a chief of the Northern Sioux, his brother-in-law, Man Afraid of His Horses, told him one day that the Sioux made war on the whites because of the route on the Powder River; it would be better therefore to abandon this route as soon as possible.

"You speak of the disappearance of the buffalo and the other animals of the prairies," Black Foot added, "but in my country we have an abundance of buffalo, deer, elk, and antelope, many beavers on the small streams, many fish, good fish, in all our rivers. You want to have our country for nothing; that is not fair dealing. I come today to ask you today for payment for a part of my lands on which you are living. And you speak of making treaties! You have not observed the one you signed on Horse Creek. First pay us what you owe us, and then you may speak of concluding another treaty!" Here commissioner Taylor and Generals Harney and Sanborn could not refrain from declaring that for ten years the indemnities due the Indians had been regularly

[5] The forts along the Powder River route were Fort Reno, Fort Phil Kearny, and Fort C. F. Smith.

115

sent from Washington; if they had not arrived, it was because the agents had stolen them.[6] "We are ashamed of that," said the commissioners to the Indians, "but justice will be done."

Nevertheless, the Wolf followed Black Foot and said that it would be the easier to abandon the Powder River route because the settlers who passed that way in search of gold in Montana Territory could take either the Missouri or the route on the other side, on the left bank. "I'll give you those two routes," said the Wolf, "but not the others. There is much gold in my country. I know where it is, but I have never told anyone for fear the whites would invade the area. We have no need of gold or silver, we do not use it in our exchange. Those who need it can take one of the two routes I have indicated. I give them to you. I am hungry and I need to go home to eat buffalo. . . . Give me the gifts which you wish to give me, little or much, so that I may return. I love my country, I love my buffalo. I love my wife and children and I wish to see them again. . . . You say you will give horses to the family of the chief who disappeared among you; I truly hope that you will give them to all of us, so that we may all return on horseback. I have spoken."

Scarcely had the Wolf finished when an old sachem arose, made the rounds of the half-circle of the commissioners, shaking the hand of each, and said that he had a long journey before him to return, and that he did not want to leave without the good wishes of his white fathers. The commissioners wished him the happiest of journeys.

The treaty of peace was then unrolled and presented to the Crows for their signatures, but none of them wished to sign.[7] Some said they

[6] Not only do most of the agents steal the items sent to the tribes, but even sell them again to the Indians at double or triple their value. At other times the government in Washington, itself deceived by its agents, sends objects of no usefulness, such as hundreds of dozens of elastic garters to a people who wear no stockings, or forks to people who eat with their fingers, or again chests of jews-harps, little mirrors, broken jackknives, in a word, all the unsalable goods of the shops of New York, Philadelphia, or Baltimore, which have been sold at a high price to the central government, and which the Indians can have no use for. Everywhere, from north to south in the United States, similar scandalous dealings have been noted not only by Indian chiefs, who have frequently complained bitterly, but also by government inquiries themselves. [*Simonin's note.*]

[7] Indians sign by making a cross, a pen stroke, or an effort to sketch the animal whose name they bear: the bear, the wolf, the deer, the tortoise, etc. [*Simonin's note.*]

could not do so without the consent of the Sioux, who were not present; others, that they would not sign unless the routes and forts of the Powder River were first abandoned, the object of all their discussions. The Wolf added that not all the Crow chiefs were present, and that they had not made known their wishes. In short, the failure was complete, though results had been so decisive with the five great nations of the South; and the commissioners saw themselves forced to postpone the renewal of their labors to a more propitious time and a more favorable season. They agreed on a conference "in seven moons, when the grass will be green," which in the calendar of civilized people signified toward the fifth of June, 1868. The place of rendezvous this time would be Fort Phil Kearny and no longer Fort Laramie. This satisfied the Crows, who gain several hundred miles on the way. Finally, it was announced to the chiefs, who were impatient to receive their gifts and be on their way, that the gifts had arrived and that there were many fine ones, to which the Crows responded with grunts of pleasure; and the meeting was adjourned.

Last evening the commissioners also held a powwow with the two Arapaho chiefs, Sorrel Horse and Black Coal. The interpreter was Friday, an Arapaho, who had been found as a small child on the prairies by Major Fitzpatrick, one of the most famous traders of the West.[8] The child had been found on a Friday, hence the name given him, like that of Robinson Crusoe's faithful servant. The Major had had the child brought up; then, when his adopted son reached twenty years of age, returned him to his tribe. Friday speaks English fluently, but does not write it, for he has profited but little by the education which the Major provided for him. Today he lives with the Arapahos, for whom he is interpreter and agent. He is of the tribal type, his glance insincere, his air deceitful, and there is no comparison between

[8] Majoı Thomas Fitzpatrick (1799–1854), trapper, trader, mountain man, and Indian agent, had been in the West for more than thirty years and was regarded by the Indians as a fair agent. Friday, who returned to live with his people after attending school in St. Louis, was for many years an interpreter and acted as a restraining influence upon his tribe. It was Friday who in 1869 asked that the Arapahos be transferred to the Wind River Reservation in Wyoming, where he subsequently lived until his death. His story is told in Appendix A to LeRoy Hafen and W. J. Ghent, *Broken Hand, the Life Story of Thomas Fitzpatrick* (Denver: Old West Publishing Co., 1931).

the broad, open, majestic physiognomy of the Crows and that of the Arapahos. The latter have been in recent years, along with the Cheyennes, the bloodiest of the prairie Indians, and their type, to judge by the three I have seen, who singularly resembled each other, corroborates their terrible reputation. They are men whom one would not care to meet alone in the recesses of some forest. This antipathy, the repulsion even, of the whites toward this frightening band of Redskins does not arise from the language of the Arapahos alone, a language obscure in sound, wholly guttural, and impossible of reproduction in the sounds of our own language.

Sorrel Horse spoke before the commissioners in the name of his entire tribe, camped between the North and the South Platte. Little Shield, the great chief, had made him his deputy. The orator's air seemed to suggest a speech strewn with invectives and filled with malice, like the one Black Foot had delivered the night before, though otherwise a just complaint. But it was nothing of the sort. The speech was most calm. Sorrel Horse spoke sitting, and discussed the needs of his tribe with the commissioners as one might speak of his affairs after dinner, with his family:

"Today," he said, "I have done what I have wished to do for a long time, I have shaken the hands of my white fathers, whom I love. . . . As soon as I knew you were asking for me, I hastened. Our old sachems have sent me to you, and they await with impatience the report I shall bring them. . . . South of the Platte there are excellent lands, well watered; that is where we wish to establish ourselves and to begin to cultivate the land. That is why I have come to you. Build me a house where I may pass my life. Teach me to plant the wheat and corn. . . . What you have done for the Arapahos of the South is good, and I think you will do the same for those of the North. . . . Little Wolf and Old Bear, chief of the Cheyennes of the North, and Man Afraid of His Horses, who commands a band of the Sioux, came to see me, and congratulated me on the journey I was about to make, and said that they, too, wished to come to visit you. . . . At the next moon, I wish to go with some of my men to plant my tent south of the Platte, near Fort Sanders.[9] It makes little difference to me if the snow is deep. My tribe

[9] Fort Sanders, established in July, 1866, for the protection of railroad tie cutters and crews, was located two miles south of the present city of Laramie, Wyoming.

will come and join me in the spring. . . . I shall need some provisions from you when I change camp. . . . I must hunt to live. I have very little powder left, and you would please me by giving me some. . . . Our old sachems will also ask me for tobacco when I return. I have finished."

The commission replied to the words of Sorrel Horse by giving him all he asked. The Arapahos left satisfied, and the commissioners were no less so at finding any Indians so conciliatory.

The northern Sioux and Cheyennes, expected every day, not having appeared, the commission is about to break up. A few of them will remain at Laramie to receive the gifts which have come and to distribute them to the Indians; the rest will return to Cheyenne and from there to North Platte, to which those who remain at Laramie will themselves soon return.

CHAPTER 16

Moneka, the Pearl of the Prairies

Fort Laramie, 15 November

During my leisure moments between the councils I strolled about the fort. I love the solemn calm of this desert. Lines of low hills run in all directions in the country around, hills formed of soft sandstone and rounded pebbles, such as I have several times described. At the foot of one of these knolls are cottonwoods, or Canadian poplars, bordering on the waters of a small stream. This is the Redskins' cemetery, for the Indians are shrouded in the branches of these trees. The body is wrapped in canvas or in a sewn buffalo skin, sometimes in a woolen blanket, and the corpse is placed there with his finest ornaments, his decorated moccasins, his necklaces of shells or glass trinkets. Wolves and starving predators violate these sepulchers, as one may easily verify by climbing the trees. The linen which covers the body is often torn to shreds by animals, and the bones of the skeleton do not retain their normal position. Nevertheless, some bodies remain well preserved and protected by the outer envelope, and I have seen one of a young woman whose skin was still intact and even still kept its color. The pure air of the prairies had mummified this delicate form, and you would say that life had scarcely departed or that the young Indian girl was still sleeping.

I asked Swift Bear why the Indians shrouded their dead thus in the open air instead of placing them in the earth. "The spirits like to travel," he answered, "especially at night; we must put no obstacles

120

in their way, and the earth which you throw on them prevents them from coming out."

It is no doubt to facilitate such journeys that they often place the saddle of the dead man's horse on his tomb. A Sioux chief was so buried in the midst of the prairie at Fort Laramie, Old Smoke, or, as the traders of the region called him, Father Laboucane. The saddle is on the grave, and so great is the Indian respect for tombs that no one has yet stolen it.

These dead, silent hosts of the Great Plains are not the only ones buried near Fort Laramie. Other dead sleep in this flat country; the cemetery at the fort has offered a last asylum to more than one emigrant, and more than one soldier has found his last resting place on the distant prairies. The stones here tell of more than one doleful incident. Death has brought together ranks, and races even, for some Indians are buried in the white cemetery, though with their own mode of burial. These coffins, supported on four stilts, are covered with a red blanket. One particularly attracts attention. A horse's head is nailed to each of the supports, and on the opposite uprights the tails are fastened. Scattered on the ground in front of the heads one observes the staves of a small keg which has been broken into pieces. What do these emblems signify? Is it the tomb of a great chief, and did they sacrifice there the two ponies which he most cherished, after the manner of the ancient German warriors?

I learned from a resident of the fort the history which accompanies this tomb. "It is not a chief's tomb," he said. "It is the tomb of Moneka, the daughter of Spotted Tail."[1]

"I have heard of Spotted Tail and his reputation," I answered. "Who could be ignorant of the name of Sintegeleshka, the famous chief of the Brulés? However, I have never seen him."

---

[1] The tale of Moneka finds its origin in the report of Colonel Henry E. Maynadier, then commandant of Fort Laramie, of March 9, 1866, as it appeared in the *Report of the Commissioner of Indian Affairs for the Year 1866* (Washington: G.P.O., 1866), No. 87, pp. 207–208. Captain Eugene F. Ware, who was stationed at Fort Laramie at the same time, gives a more realistic account of Spotted Tail's daughter in Appendix A of *The Indian War of 1864* (Lincoln: University of Nebraska Press, 1960). Maynadier does not mention the girl by name, and Ware calls her Ah-ho-ap-pa; it is not clear where Simonin found the name Moneka. Neither Maynadier nor Ware mentions a romance between the girl and a white officer.

"What! You have never seen Spotted Tail and you have come to the prairies?"

"I have not yet seen Sintegeleshka. The first time I took the Pacific railroad, a few weeks ago, the great warrior was in the neighborhood of Fort Sedgwick, near the station of Julesburg. We were told that he was again on bad terms with the whites, and that he would stop the train, as his braves had already recently done."

"And he derailed you?"

"Nothing of the sort happened. Spotted Tail even exchanged a friendly greeting with the commissioners at North Platte, and promised them to appear at the council at Fort Laramie, together with his warriors."

"You notice that he did not come."

"I see that all too well. Therefore, since I cannot hear the story of Moneka from his mouth, I beg of you to tell it to me."

My interlocutor yielded with good grace to my request, and told me the story of Moneka. Here it is, faithfully, as I took it from his mouth.

Moneka (in Sioux, the Pearl of the Prairies) was the only daughter of Spotted Tail. Three years ago her father was at war with the whites. Moneka followed her father and camped with him in the neighborhood of Fort Laramie. There she fell in love with a young officer of the fort; and since she had always wished to marry a paleface, she asked her father's permission to be the wife of the officer. The chief angrily refused his consent and departed with his braves and all his warriors to the farthest edge of the prairies, four hundred miles to the east. He left death and desolation everywhere on his path, attacked wagon trains, burned farms, and killed whites without pity, carrying their scalps with him like so many trophies. This continued for a whole year, and the name of Spotted Tail became the terror of the prairies.

Meanwhile, Moneka, who did not wish to disobey her father, became sad and silent. She who used to bring so much gaiety into the Indian camp, who always began the dances and the songs, now remained melancholy for more than a year, speaking not a word to anyone, even to Spotted Tail. Little by little she wasted away with the illness. One day, feeling her strength at an end, she caused the great chief to be summoned.

"My father," she said, "I am dying. You know that I have always loved the whites. I ask to rest in their cemetery. Make peace with the palefaces; they are stronger than we are. They are already masters of half the prairies, and the Indian will disappear before them. Promise me that you will make peace, and that you will bury me in the white cemetery at Laramie."

These were the last words of Moneka, who died in the arms of her desolated father. All the tribe mourned her death, for all loved her, and the old trader, Pallardy, who had known the young princess, said to me just now in his own quaint speech, "She was a fine, sensitive girl, and reasoned well; what a pity that she is not still alive!"

The day after Moneka's death Spotted Tail called all his warriors together, and in one of those speeches which the Indians are so skilled at improvising, told them with moving eloquence of the last moments of his daughter.

"I wish to carry out her last wishes," he said; "we are leaving for Fort Laramie and we shall take Moneka's body there."

And then all these men, without a word, mounted their horses and followed their chief. Spotted Tail himself carried the body of his daughter.[2] For five days they journeyed in this manner. On the sixth they finally came to Laramie.

As the Redskins were at war with the whites, Spotted Tail caused his band to stop at some distance from the fort, then asked for an interview with the commandant, Colonel Maynadier, who granted his request.

"Father," he said, "I come here to you to fulfill a duty. I bring the body of my daughter, who, as she was dying, asked me to promise that she be buried at Fort Laramie."

The commander, moved, promised Spotted Tail to accept the body of Moneka and to bury it with all the ceremonies that the whites practice on such occasions. The chaplain of the fort was immediately notified; and the following day, just as the great chief of the Brulés, followed by his warriors, came to deliver the body of Moneka into the hands of the commandant, he was met at the gate of the cemetery by Colonel Maynadier himself and his officers in full uniform. Beside

[2] Captain Ware says the two ponies carried the body on an improvised litter.

him were the chaplain and his assistants and the various employees and residents of the fort. A detachment of soldiers formed a line. The Indians came on horseback, clothed in their finest costumes.

Services for the dead were intoned according to Christian rites, and the fort interpreter translated each verse for the Redskins. The children of the desert were profoundly moved, never having heard in their own language the chant of a poetry so austere, so somber. For the first time they shed tears.

Then came the moment of the offerings. It is the Indian custom at the burial of one's dead to say a final farewell and to give a present. The commandant removed his gloves. "I give these gloves to the beautiful Moneka," he said, "that she may cover her hands and protect them against the cold on the long journey which she will make toward the happy plains."

The Indians came next, each offering to the Pearl of the Prairies whatever he had most precious.

Finally, Moneka was placed in a coffin of cedar wood, which was raised on four posts in a corner of the fort's cemetery. Upon it was thrown a covering of red wool, the color preferred by the Indians. The two ponies which she rode by preference were killed on the tomb of the young princess, and their heads nailed to the posts which supported her head, and their tails where her feet lay. In front of the heads a small cask of water was placed, so that the horses might quench their thirst on their long journey toward the happy plains, toward the prairies where it is always fair weather, and where the buffalo may be hunted without ever any fatigue.

And this is how, if you ever visit Fort Laramie, you will hear the tale of Moneka, Pearl of the Prairies, daughter of Spotted Tail.[3]

[3] In 1876 Spotted Tail removed his daughter's body from Fort Laramie to the Black Hills Agency.

CHAPTER 17

The Savages

Camp on Chug Creek, on the prairies of Dakota, 16 November

We are on our way back to Cheyenne, halfway between Fort Laramie and that city. We are returning by a different route,[1] which reminds me of the adage of an old traveler who told me that one must never pass twice by the same route if one wishes always to see something new. Something new! We have seen plenty these days, and we shall see more, as much as one could wish.

I took Pallardy into my covered wagon, and he agreed to leave his three sachems for a while and to give me a few more details on the savages, the "red devils" of the prairies. He is particularly fond of the Sioux, and among them Fast Bear, the wisest, most respected of the great chiefs. Fast Bear is a friend of the whites and loses no opportunity to advise his band to live in peace with the palefaces. "For a man with no education he gives them good advice," said Pallardy. "He is the wisest of the Sioux, and what an orator!"

With the aid of this good interpreter I continue to enlarge my French-Sioux vocabulary. As you might suppose, there are numerous words which have no direct equivalent in the Indian languages; in such case, the Indians make use of some circumlocution. And since these terms generally refer to things which the savages have always regarded as

---

[1] The different route, judging from the Chug Creek address, would appear to be roughly the later Cheyenne-Chugwater-Fort Laramie-Deadwood stage route (from 1876 on).

mysterious, especially where they have never seen them, for example, brandy, the steamboat, firearms, the Indians designate these, respectively, as magic water, magic canoe, magic fire. Do you know how the traders have always translated the word mystery or magic? By *medicine*. The French-Canadians, the first *coureurs* of the prairies, conceived the custom of calling the witch doctors, the soothsayers, and the tribal doctors all *medicine men* (doctors). The word has remained. It has also passed into English, and today, among the Indians on the prairies, one hears only of *medicine* and *medicine men*. The Manitou, the Great Spirit himself, has become the Medicine Man par excellence. The horse is the magic dog, the *medicine dog*, as the traders say. You can invent further examples yourself.

The Indians, who do not suspect in what whimsical fashion the whites have translated their metaphors, have other very pretty ones. Thus they call the moon the sun of night; leaves, the hair of the trees; fingers, children of the hand, etc.

The savage method of computing is the most logical possible, and would delight our professors of arithmetic. The Sioux and most of the Indians begin by counting to ten. Eleven is ten and one; twelve, ten and two; and so on to twenty, which is called ten-ten. Then they begin again at two-ten and one, two-ten and two, and so on up to three-ten, which is thirty, up to ten-ten, which is one hundred. This continues indefinitely. In a minute, the time it takes to write the first ten figures, you have your lesson in spoken enumeration, and that is it. As for written enumeration, that does not exist. The savages do not write; at most, they trace some designs on skins. These are the figures of men, animals, and some crude representations of battles. This is what scholars call *pictographic* writing. Since it has always a single meaning, you might say that it is a sort of hieroglyph. But do not try to compare it with the Egyptian; caricatures, the formless sketches which young students make in their notebooks, alone can give an idea of Indian pictography.

Like all primitive peoples, the Indians count their months by moons. As for years, they pay little attention to that. They give the months names which correspond to the phenomena of vegetation or climate, or again with the different stages of the bison with which they live.

January is the month of the cold moon; February, the month when

126

the female of the bison is large; March, the month when the snow melts or the grass comes up; April, the moon of the green grass; May, the month when the female of the bison gives birth; June, the month when the little bison begin to run; July, the berries turn red (in our countryside we say the month of cherries). August is the month of fruits; September, the bison has all his fur; October, the young bison (the savages' veal) are good to eat; November, the bison's fur is black; and December is the time to prepare the bison hides. The cold moon soon begins.

These names of the months I wrote under the dictation of Pallardy. They vary very little from tribe to tribe and, as you see, are fairly long. But there is no written calendar here, and no need to economize on words for months otherwise always too brief, as are the lunar months.

I asked Pallardy to give me some lessons in the Indian sign language. "But it is nearly the same as that of your deaf-mutes," he said.

"Good. However, I do not know that either, being neither deaf nor mute."

"Well, you must learn that when the Indians speak, they make all the gestures to accompany the words, or that correspond with the idea being expressed. You remember that Fast Bear said to me the other day as we left the Laramie council that he understood the Crows entirely by the gestures which accompanied their speeches."

"But what are these gestures, Pallardy?"

"That would take too long to tell you."

"Anyway, give me some examples, the most common ones."

"All right, if you wish. To indicate the Sioux, all the tribes make the sign of cutting the throat with the hand; for the Cheyennes, the sign of cutting the arm several times. For the Arapahos, you seize the nose with the thumb and index finger, as if the Arapahos smelled bad. For the Comanches, of whom the Snakes are a part, you move the index finger horizontally as if showing the movement of the snake. For the Crows, you agitate the hands in imitation of the flight of birds; and for the Pawnees, who include the Wolf tribe, you put the hands behind the ears to round them and make them stand up like the wolf's ears. You see, then, how, when the Indians happen to meet on the prairies, they know at once with whom they are dealing and how to behave in consequence."

127

"That is well imagined. Are there some other signs, in such cases?"

"Certainly. If you are a white man meeting some Indians coming toward you on the prairie, raise your right hand, as if you were taking an oath. The Indians will understand that you mean for them to halt."

"And then?"

"Then move your lifted hand from right to left and left to right. That means, Who are you? I do not know you."

"I see. Then the Indians will give me one of the signs you just showed me."

"If you do not understand their answer, you can lift both hands in the air, holding them together and shaking them as if shaking hands. That means, Are you friends? You can also raise the two hands separately, closing them and holding up the two index fingers. This sign has the same meaning. If the Indians are friendly they will reply with the same sign as yours."

"And if they are enemies?"

"Then they will come right toward you without halting, putting their horses to the gallop; or, holding the hand closed, they will press it against the forehead, turning it several times from the side of the palm to the back, which means, Be on your guard, we are enemies and at war."

"Thank you, Pallardy; I shall make use of this dictionary if the occasion arises."

"We old traders know all that like our *Pater Noster*, from father to son; there is no danger of our making a mistake."

"Now tell me, Pallardy, is it true that the Indians have also a telegraphic language? I have been told that they light fires on the mountains to communicate at a distance, like our ancient Gauls."

"I can't tell you about the ancient Gauls; I have never been among them. But I know that the Redskins have a telegraph and use it on occasion."

"And how do they do that?"

"Here's how: you know that the air is so pure and transparent on the prairies that you can see some objects a hundred miles distant. The Indians light fires at night on the hills or use smoke in the daytime. The number and the placing of the fires or the smokes, the interval,

128

the time left between them, have meanings which they know in advance. Enemies or strangers have been seen in the country, the bison have come, or perhaps a band returning from war or a distant hunting party is announcing its return, and the like."

"Give me an example."

" Well, if someone has just discovered the approach of an enemy, supposing it is daytime, a smoke signal given off twice at fifteen-minute intervals indicates that the enemy is not great in number, and three times, with the same intervals, that the enemy is advancing in strength."

"And how do they provide these smoke signals?"

"By lighting dry wood and throwing on it green branches of pine and other trees or resinous plants."

It was partly on your account that I got Pallardy to talk. I learned some new things from him, you see, and send you my notes from this camp without delay, before I forget them. I might have told you what so many others have written of the Redskins before me, what everyone knows; but I preferred to let the old trader talk, and write you from the honest old trapper's dictation, as it were. Pallardy has taught me most of the little I know of the Redskins. He has lived for thirty years among these savages, these barbarians, as he still calls them. What doesn't he know about them, what hasn't he learned from them? He has even learned to scalp; he has even scalped alive, and just gave me a lesson, theoretical, of course, on the subject.

"What, Pallardy, you yourself have scalped your neighbor?"

"Well, monsieur, one has to howl with the wolves. I was with the Sioux, in war with the Cheyennes, who had stolen everything from us. I was thoroughly beaten. After the fight I did like the rest, I scalped. You get a good grip on your knife, you make a circle all around the sinciput, as you call it; you pull, and it comes off by itself. It is no more difficult than that."

"And why take the enemy's scalp?"

"That's their decoration, the savages. The one who has taken a lot of scalps has a good chance to be named chief of his tribe, as you might say mayor of a town. It's a proof of courage because you have to have killed your enemy before you scalp him. Some tribes shave their heads, but they take pains to leave a tuft of hair on top, in case one

129

should happen to fall in battle. One mustn't cheat the victor of this; that's one of the laws of savage chivalry."

Thus the Canadian brought me up to date on the manners and customs of the prairies.

Do what you will with this long dissertation. As for me, I have reached the end of Pallardy's confidences. But I still shiver: "It comes off by itself!"

CHAPTER 18

The Indian Question

Permit me to speak a little further on the Redskin.

The great powwow at Fort Laramie describes clearly and precisely their present situation vis-a-vis the whites. These latter have at all times recognized the Indians' right to possession of the land; but also, obeying the inexorable law which pushes colonists toward the west, they have always known that they must dispossess the Indian of these prairies which the savages love so deeply. No doubt treaties have sanctioned and legitimized the dispossession, and the price for the land has been paid to the Indian in gifts and in money. But it would not be difficult to relate how the agents of the United States steal these gifts en route. It would be easy to cite names, if necessary, and to estimate the fortunes which certain agents who have been assigned to the Far West have accumulated in a very few years. True, they are poorly paid, since they receive but a thousand to fifteen hundred dollars a year (five to eight thousand francs at most), in a country where everything is scarce and living is dear. Instead of demanding a better stated pay from the central government, they prefer to rob the State and at the same time the Indian. When the gifts arrive for the Redskin, they have often been so selected as to be almost unusable, or made up of already spoiled merchandise. Has not the Redskin reason to complain and often to avenge himself against such indignities?

131

But this is only a primary cause of the sullen war between the native savage and the immigrant white.

They tell the Redskin: "Colonization pushes us toward the farthest West, toward which we advance every day a bit more; we need a part of your land, and you will remain in the rest, with boundaries strictly defined. There you can cultivate the soil." To which the savage, as you will have seen, replies in anger that the prairies are his, that he was born to hunt the buffalo, and that working the earth, as he is advised to do, is not at all his affair. A tradition runs through the Indian peoples that their race will disappear the day when there are no more buffalo. So when it is proposed to confine them in reservations, threatening at the same time to put them there by force, some of them answer, "We would rather die from a bullet than from hunger." Still, it would be a mistake to assume that all the Indians are thus rebels against confinement.

Fast Bear, the Sioux chief, says he will plow this winter with his men, and you heard Sorrel Horse, the Arapaho, ask the commissioners of the Union, in his last speech, to build him a farm near the Platte. You know, too, how the five great nations of the South have accepted the reservations which have recently been assigned to them; but, on the other hand, you recall with what disdain the Crows replied to the proposal of the commissioners that they confine themselves to a portion of their territory and there cultivate the soil. Most of the bands into which the great Sioux nation is subdivided share the horror of the Crows at the peaceful toil of agriculture. The young Redskins and adolescent warriors are especially outstanding for the opposition to the white proposals.

The old chiefs, the ancients of the tribes, often say in the councils held with the United States commissioners, "We are willing to go on the reservations and to live in peace with you, but we cannot answer for our young men."

They are a strange race, these Redskins, to whom nature has assigned the most beautiful soil on earth, rich in alluvial deposits, deep and level and well watered; and yet this race has not yet emerged from the primitive stage which the human race has always known at the beginning of its evolution, that of a hunting, nomadic people, the age of stone! If the whites had not brought them iron, the Indians would still be armed with flint, like the antediluvian man who peopled Europe a hundred thousand years ago and lived in caves. The Indians flee from work, aside from hunting and warfare; the women do all the work among them. What a contrast to the race which surrounds them, so industrious, so busy, and with such a profound respect for women. This race hems them in, entirely surrounds them today, and the Redskin's day is over if he does not consent to retire to the reservations.

And even on the reservations, will industry and the arts appear? The red race is the most poorly endowed in music and song. The fine arts, among them, are still in their infancy. Writing, aside from a crude pictographic representation, is entirely unknown. They barely know how to trace a few designs in beads on hides. These designs are undoubtedly often happily grouped and the colors blended in a certain harmony, but that is all. Apart from a rudimentary preparation of meats and the tanning of skins and furs, their industry is equally negligible. The Indian is less advanced than the African negro, who at least knows how to weave and dye cloth. The Navahos of New Mexico are the only Redskins who manufacture woolen blankets.

It is estimated that there are around a hundred thousand free Indians on the prairies, scattered between the Missouri and the Rocky Mountains. The number of all the Indians of North America [i.e., in the United States], from the Atlantic to the Pacific, is estimated at four hundred thousand. Perhaps this figure is a little short. Statistics, exact information, are wholly lacking. The Indians themselves never give more than the number of their tents or lodges, but a lodge contains a number of different individuals, according to the tribe and sometimes in the same tribe; hence the impossibility of exact estimates.

On the northern prairies we must note especially the great nation of the Sioux, who number thirty-five thousand. The Crows, the Gros Ventres, the Blackfeet, etc., who occupy in particular the territories of Idaho and Montana, represent all together a population figure of less than that of the Sioux, perhaps twenty thousand. In the center and the South, the Pawnees, the Arapahos, the Cheyennes, the Utes, the Kiowas, the Commanches, the Apaches, etc., all together exceed the figure of forty thousand. These bands roam over the territories of

Nebraska, Kansas, Colorado, Texas, and New Mexico. The Pawnees are on reservations in Nebraska, in the neighborhood of the Pacific railroad, and the Utes in the high "parks" of Colorado. All these tribes have certain characteristics in common; they are nomadic, that is, live in no fixed place, live by fishing and especially by hunting, and follow the buffalo in all his migrations.

An absolutely democratic mode of living and a sort of communal life determine all relationships between members of the same tribe toward one another. The chiefs are named by election and for a certain time. Nevertheless, they are sometimes hereditary. The most courageous, the one who has taken the most scalps in war or who has killed the most buffalo, he who has done some outstanding deed, he who speaks with great eloquence, all such have a right to be chiefs. So long as a chief conducts himself well, he retains his rank; should he forfeit esteem, another chief is named. The chiefs lead the war parties and are consulted in difficult times; so are the old men. The chief's lieutenants, the "braves," are second in command in time of war. There is no judge in the tribe; each determines his own justice and applies the law as he sees it.

All the tribes hunt and make war in the same manner, on horseback, with the lance and the bow and arrows, when they lack revolvers and rifles. They have a shield to defend themselves against the blows of an enemy. They live entirely off the buffalo and clothe themselves with this animal's skin, which they tan with its brains. They scalp the dead enemy and deprive him of his hair. They pillage and devastate farms, make captives of women and children, and often submit those who fall into their hands alive to frightful tortures before killing them. The squaws to whom they deliver their prisoners show a revolting cruelty toward them. You have heard how they snatch out the eyes, the tongue, the nails of the victim; burn him, cut off a hand one day, a foot another. When they have thoroughly tortured the captive, they light a coal fire on his stomach and dance howling around him. Almost all the Redskins commit atrocities toward the whites as soon as they go to war with them.

The tribes often make war on the slightest pretext, over a herd of buffalo which they are following or a prairie where they wish to camp alone. They have no reserved places, it is true, but they sometimes wish to keep one to themselves to the exclusion of any other. Indeed, it is not uncommon that the same tribe breaks up into two enemy clans. A few years ago the Oglalas, drunk on whiskey, fought among themselves with rifle shots, and since then separated into two bands, the Bad Faces, commanded by Red Cloud, and the other by Big Mouth and Pawnee Killer.

The languages of these tribes are all different, though perhaps a skilled linguist would recognize common roots among them, such as have been discovered in our day among the languages of Europe and India. The Indian languages obey the same grammatical mechanism: they are *agglutinative* or *polysynthetic* and not *analytic* or *inflected* (forgive me for using these italicized terms), that is to say, for example, that in their language words may combine with one another to form a single word expressing a complete idea to which each of the composing words contributes; but matters of relationship, gender, number, are not shown by any modification, notably of the noun. These languages do not have, or appear not to have, any affinity in the different terms of their vocabulary, which is, for that matter, often very limited.

To make themselves understood with one another, the tribes have adopted by common agreement the language of signs or gestures, which I have already described. By these means all the Indians understand one another, and a Ute, for example, can easily carry on a conversation for several hours with an Arapaho, and he with a Sioux, etc. Besides this language of signs, the Indians have also a telegraphic language among them, which you also know.

Other usages are common to all the Redskins. They practice polygamy and commonly beat their women, and yet they all show the greatest affection for their children. One day a Colorado miner asked a Ute if he would sell his daughter, a little child with a lively eye, full of intelligence, who spoke Spanish well.

"Do your people sell their children?" the Ute answered proudly.

"No," said the white, a little surprised.

"Well, neither do we; keep your money."

A certain spirit of chivalry, like the love of children, is one of the distinctive traits of the Redskin. Not that the savage keeps his word strictly, or will not steal from you, or kill you if need be to take what

135

you have. But he shows great courage in war, he loves combat, and he does not have to be stirred to war by the smell of powder, or by martial music or by strong liquor. He faces danger everywhere. Furthermore, material interests are never his preoccupation; he has no care for yours and mine, and you have seen how little he makes of gold, for which, indeed, he has no need.

Nor shall I ever forget, among the traits common to all Indians, the continual practice of the art of oratory, producing such remarkable and such eloquent improvisers. No more shall I forget the deep-rooted hatred for the white which characterizes the red, shared by the very women, on all occasions. The first tribes encountered by the whites along the Atlantic could hardly have loved them any more, as you may judge by the following incident: I met a Delaware princess one day in New York, dressed in half-white, half-Indian fashion, and very becomingly. Her features were Indian, but she spoke English so well that I allowed myself to ask her if she were of mixed blood. She looked at me proudly: "I am a Delaware," she said, "and proud of it. Not a drop of foreign blood is mingled with the blood of my people. The whites took my lands and paid not a hundredth part of their value. I hate the whites who stole my country." And opening her shawl, which hid a bodice of fur on which a wolf had been embroidered, she said, "The wolf is the emblem of the Delawares, and I shall never forget it. The Great Spirit has punished us by bringing the whites among us, but I shall never lose the memory of my country and my ancestors."

All Redskins believe in a superior being, the Manitou, or Great Spirit, who created and rules all things. They believe also in the immortality of the soul and in a reward for the good and punishment for the wicked after this life. "Over there, toward the rising sun, lie the happy prairies," said a Sioux to me one day. "The path which leads to it is long and hard. When one has been just and good in this life, this is the path he takes. The wicked take another. The starting place is the same, but the two paths go farther and farther apart."

According to Indian theogony, which, as you might guess, is very obscure, the Great Spirit manifests himself in various ways and may divide into two. There are even several different spirits, Thunder, Wind, for example; finally certain animals even, like the beloved buffalo, serve as a residence for these spirits and have a soul like men.

The legends and traditions which the Redskins have retained on their coming to, or appearance in, America are scarcely more precise than those of their theogony. They say they came from the north or the west, by sea, but often they do not say this of themselves; it has been put into their mouths. You know how linguists and anthropologists customarily associate the North American peoples with those of Asia, the anthropologist by certain cranial characteristics, the linguists by certain terms in their languages. A few even, who swear only by the Bible, a book which should be kept closed in such matters, argue that the Redskins descend directly from the Jews and think they can prove it.[1] The Jews would have had to cross all central Asia and leap the Bering Strait in one of their exoduses.

While certain ethnologists link the Redskins with Asiatic peoples, others derive at least certain tribes among them from European races. This time the Redskins would have had to come from the east, always by sea. A few even argue that the Mandans, whose traces may be followed from the mouth of the Mississippi to the point on the upper Missouri where their extinction begins, are no more than degenerated Gauls. These would have had to emigrate from Gallic lands in the eighth century of our era, others say some centuries later, under the leadership of one of their chiefs, Madoc.[2] Would a few common roots

[1] It is said that the Puritan John Eliot, who labored to put the Bible into Indian language, suggested the possibility that the Indians were descended from the lost tribes of Israel. James Adair, an Irish-born American who lived among the Chickasaws and Cherokees from 1735 to 1770, wrote *A History of the American Indians* (1775) for the purpose of advancing this theory. He was supported by Elias Boudinot, once president of the Continental Congress, in a book entitled *A Star in the West* (1816). Thomas Jefferson, however, explicitly rejected the idea of the Jewish origin of the Indians. In a letter to John Adams (June 11, 1812), he wrote: "Adair too had his kink. He believed all the Indians of America to be descended from the Jews . . . and that they all spoke Hebrew." (*The Adams-Jefferson Letters*, ed. Lester J. Capon [Chapel Hill: University of North Carolina Press, 1959], II, 306.)

[2] The legend of the Mandans as white-skinned, blue-eyed Indians descended from the Welsh arose from an ancient legend that the Welsh prince Madoc, about 1170, sailed the Atlantic, discovered America, and later returned with a party of colonists, who disappeared somewhere in the West. The London Welsh raised money for an expedition and in 1792 sent John Evans to America to investigate reports that the Mandans were descended from these colonists. His visit to the Mandans convinced him that they were not Welsh, and indeed, that no Indians were Welsh. See

137

in the Mandan languages and the Gaelic suffice to propose this idea—to say nothing of the journey across the sea? It is proved not only by songs and legends but also by authentic inscriptions that the Scandinavians discovered North America in the ninth or tenth centuries of our era—a century is of no great significance here.

Whatever there may be to all these unproved theories, which neither linguistics nor ethnology nor anthropology has satisfactorily unraveled, it is certain that all Redskins share certain common characteristics, even in the type. At the same time, one cannot forget that there are significant differences on a number of points. Thus the prairie Indian is certainly more warlike than the California Indian, and the Arapahos are not of the same type as the Sioux or the Crows. Again, the Indians do not all build their dwellings in the same way, and the form of these often serves to identify the tribe.

I have said that the traditions of the Redskins relative to their coming to America have been erased, and that on this subject they often say only what scholars have taught them to say. Let me give you one of the most convincing illustrations: A few days ago I came on Commissioner Taylor in conversation with Fast Bear. Our caravan was camped at Lone Tree Creek, on the way to Laramie. Fires had been lighted, and all, under the starry vault of the sky, had freely joined in the conversation of the bivouac. Fast Bear is surely one of the most intelligent Indians of the prairie; furthermore, he is good and humane, and one day when his tribe was at war with the whites, he himself carried a wounded soldier on his back as far as Fort Laramie and saved his life. This act of generosity, which would have moved the moralists of ancient Greece and Rome, rounds out the portrait of Fast Bear and deserves to

---

Bernard De Voto, *The Course of Empire* (Boston: Houghton Mifflin, 1952), pp. 373–379.

Nevertheless, the story persisted, and when Lewis and Clark encountered the Flathead Indians, Clark recorded (September 5, 1805) that they spoke "a gurgling kind of language . . . the strangest language of any we have ever seen. . . . We take these savages to be the Welsh Indians if there be any such from the language. So Captain Lewis took down the names of everything in their language in order that it may be found out whether they are or whether they sprang or originated first from the Welsh or not." (*The Journals of Lewis and Clark*, ed. Bernard De Voto [Boston: Houghton Mifflin, 1953], p. 234. Clark's spelling has here been modernized.)

be commemorated. It was this man, first in all respects among the Sioux, whose opinions I had sought to probe on the origins of his tribe. I joined in on the conversation with President Taylor, and asked the interpreter Pallardy to interrogate Fast Bear on what I wanted to know. The Bear replied that he knew nothing of the origin of the Sioux, and that his grandfathers had taught him nothing and transmitted nothing on the subject. The same answer was given me by other chiefs of the tribe; and all the traders and trappers—whose opinions, it is true, must be taken with all reservations, for the traders bother their heads very little on the subject of tribal origins—have told me that the Indians have preserved no legends and no traditions of their earliest history.

The study of the supposed cosmogonies of the Redskins should be approached with no less distrust, and all that has been advanced as to their belief in a universal flood. At the very most some tribes have preserved some vague legends referring to partial deluges, similar to those preserved in Greek mythologies. Here again writers seem most often to have written from facts supplied chiefly by their imagination. I shall give one example among a thousand. Commissioner Taylor, as a Methodist, lost no opportunity to catechize the Indians, and to speak to them of the creation of the world, the fall of Adam, the redemption of man by Christ, and many other mysteries taught by the Bible and the Gospel, of which the Indians understood hardly a drop. The other day the reverend gentleman, speaking of the creation of the world, told the Sioux that this great event took place six thousand years ago. Fast Bear, the wisest among the Sioux, meditated a moment and replied in the most innocent tone in the world: "According to my calculations, it was six thousand and ninety years." The fellow evidently was joking. How could he, who counted only by moons, have made his calculations, and what did he mean by adding ninety years to the reverend's six thousand? If some closet scholar had just happened to pass by at that moment, he would certainly have made a note of the fact, and would have written to some academy that the Sioux chronology presented a remarkable similarity to that of the Bible. You can guess the rest.

It is in some such manner as this that the history of the prairie Indians has been presented. And yet their languages are not even known, or are very badly known; it is impossible to write them with the characters and sounds to which we are accustomed.

Often there is but one interpreter for a given language, and often a poor one, and understanding only, not speaking, the language which he translates. Many, for the best of reasons, do not know how to write the language which they interpret. Neither Dr. Matthews nor John Richard nor Pierre Chêne could write for me the names of the Crow chiefs in English letters. What would it be if it were a matter of the Arapahos or the Apaches, whose excessively guttural language is stressed only on the edge of the lips? I am speaking, of course, only of the prairie tribes in all this, and not of those who formerly lived on the watersheds of the mountains which look on the Atlantic or who live along the Mississippi. Most of those tribes, as you know, are extinct, the Algonquins, the Hurons, the Iroquois, the Natchez, the Mohicans; and France, it must be admitted, contributed in large measure to that disappearance. The remnants of these tribes which I shall call Atlantic, the Delawares, the Cherokees, the Seminoles, the Osages, the Creeks, the Choctaws, are today shut up on reservations, especially in Indian Territory, where the Redskins little by little lose their distinctive traits.[3]

[3] Pushed out of Florida, the Carolinas, Georgia, and other states bordering on the Atlantic and the Mississippi, these tribes finally accepted their confinement within these boundaries. There they are practicing agriculture today, while the nomadic tribes still live by hunting, in their primitive state. They have their schoolteachers, priests, doctors, millers, and wagon-makers, originally provided by the United States, and they live in houses with roofs, while the nomadic tribes lack everything and camp here and there under tents. The Cherokees and Comanches have even an upper and lower chamber (the Kings' and the Warriors' Chambers among the Creeks). They also have newspapers and books written in their language with special characters, at least the Cherokees do. Thus a stable life little by little serves to civilize the Redskin, so much so, indeed, that in another generation it is not impossible that a state may be created out of what is now only Indian Territory. On that day the starry flag of the Union, counting already so many stars, will count one more, assuredly one of the most honorable to the American statesmen. Many of the Redskins of Indian Territory can read and write today; some have received a complete education in St. Louis or New York and are, to employ the conventional term, true *gentlemen*. Others are furthermore wealthy landed proprietors, and own a number of cultivated acres and head of cattle such as would be the envy of most of our agriculturists. The Cherokees also had slaves, like the whites, before the War of Secession. This fact indicates better than any other the stage of civilization attained by the Redskins of Indian Territory.

But histories and authenticated documents are available on all these tribes, whereas very little is known yet of the prairie tribes. Most of the legends and traditions attributed to them have been invented by travelers.

You have heard that the commissioners of the Union have recently confined the five great nations of the South in a new territory similar to the preceding, and bordering upon it. They will suggest the same sort of reservation in the north of Dakota for the Crows and the Sioux, if they find them well disposed, as is likely, in June of 1868.

And what becomes of the Indians after that, you ask? For such is the question everyone raises when there is discussion of the Redskins. If the Indians go on reservations, what has happened to those of the Atlantic coast will happen to them: they will little by little lose their customs, their savage manners, and will yield insensibly to the sedentary life of agriculture; and, the last phase, of which we have yet to witness the example, their country will little by little pass from the status of territory to that of state. Once arrived at this stage, the Indian will have entirely merged with the white; he will perhaps be no more distinct, after a few generations, than is the Frank with us from the Gaul, or the Norman from the Saxon in England.

But what if the Indian does not submit, does not consent to be restricted to the reservations? Then it is a war to the death between two races of different color and manners, a pitiless war of the sort we have so unhappily seen so frequently on the soil of America itself. Where today are the Hurons, the Iroquois, the Natchez, who so amazed our fathers? Where and how many today are the Algonquins, who did not know the limits of their empire? All have gradually disappeared from disease and war. The war that breaks out this time will be brief, and it will be the last, for the Indian will inevitably succumb to it. He has neither the science nor the numbers. No doubt he baffles formal war by his ambushes, his flight, by his isolated and totally unexpected attacks; and the most skillful strategists of the United States, General Sherman at their head, have been beaten by the Indians. The Indians have won sufficient glory against the whites. But this time it will be a war of

---

The different delegates from this territory, who may be met any winter in Washington, and the principal chiefs who rule the reservation *nations*, speak and write English fluently and have excellent manners. [*Simonin's note.*]

volunteers, and not of regulars. The pioneers of the territories will arm themselves, and if the Indian demands tooth for tooth, eye for eye, the whites in turn will impose on them the inflexible law of the talon. The tribes are clans, and like the Sardinians and Corsicans and formerly the Scotch, take revenge on a particular individual of a clan for the insult given to a member of another clan. That is why the Indian attacks any white, no matter who he is, when he has a complaint against the whites. It will be the same with volunteers. As they did at Sand Creek in Colorado, they will pursue and track down the Indian, hunt down the Redskin, until he is wiped out by numbers if he has not already submitted.

Thus the problem presents itself. One may say that it has reached its last phase, whatever the issue, and that, historically speaking, the Indian has ceased to exist. Civilization will do in a few years what smallpox and other diseases, what whiskey, firewater, not to mention white barbarities, have taken two centuries to accomplish, namely, to cut the population of the Indian in half, a population which has passed from a million to less than five hundred thousand souls from the seventeenth to the nineteenth century. In another generation there will be no more Indians. The buffalo disappears and the Indian with it, the primitive man with the primitive animal.[4]

The Pacific railroad advances victoriously across the prairies. In two years it will unite the two oceans; in two years all the states, all the territories of the Great West will be fully settled. The scenes which travelers and romancers have described will no longer exist except in books. The Indian himself will be merged with the white or will have been destroyed.

Strange destiny, that of this child of the prairies. Unwilling to bend before the law imposed on all by nature, the law of work, especially work on the soil, he will disappear without leaving a trace in the history of humanity. Strange destiny, the barbarian who will have been wiped out by civilized man, while in so many other lands it is the civilized man who has been wiped out, or, if you wish, absorbed, by the barbarian.

---

[4] The bison performs in North America the role of the auroch which formerly inhabited Europe, as the Indian of North America represents our ancestors of the age of stone and caves. [*Simonin's note.*]

CHAPTER 19

The Emancipation of Women

Pittsburgh, alias Fort Duquesne, state of Pennsylvania, 24 November

I am writing you from the state of Pennsylvania, and not from the Mormon country. The storms which we experienced in the Rocky Mountains gave me pause. I know how severe the winters are in Utah and Nevada. I should have found the Mormons and the silver mines under snow, and I should have wasted my time had I continued my way toward California, where the great winter rains would have awaited me in their turn. Note that Colonel Heine, now my sole companion, announced at Cheyenne that for his part he would go no farther and would definitely return to the East.

I took counsel with myself for a moment and, in view of the reasons I have just given, did the same. There is no use wishing to do everything at one time. We shall return next summer to visit the Latter Day Saints and the miners of Nevada and California. From San Francisco we shall have looked upon the far Orient, and we could return from this second visit, or even third, by way of Japan, China, India, Arabia, and Egypt. There would be no great merit in that. It is easier today to make the tour of the world than the tour of one's own pasture. Steam has killed the poetry and the hazards of voyages, and I understand why poets are so hostile to industry.

We shall content ourselves, therefore, on this first trip, at having covered the whole constructed length of 825 kilometres [approximately 510 miles] of the great Pacific railroad, at having visited the young

143

territory of Colorado and explored the silver and gold mines of the Rocky Mountains, and, finally, at having crossed the immense prairies of Dakota and made the acquaintance of the Redskins. That is already sufficient for a journey of less than three months; and the excursion into the Rocky Mountains, at 2,500 leagues from Paris, is surely worth as much as a trip to Switzerland.

So here I am, returned toward the civilized East.

Pittsburgh, founded by the French in the last century under the name of Fort Duquesne and taken from us by the English, is a land of iron and coal. The suburbs of this industrial city bear the names of Manchester and Birmingham and need in no way envy those two English cities for smoke and fog. But I am not writing you to describe American industry. I prefer to tell you something more of this young society, so virile, so daring, amid which I have lived for two months.

I met a curious Yankee in Cheyenne, Mr. George Francis Train, popular orator and Fenian, financier, and traveler.[1] He is involved in the operations of the Pacific railroad.

We traveled together from Cheyenne to Omaha and Chicago. At Omaha, this indefatigable excursionist, jumping from the coach long before the train had stopped, ran to the newspaper office and then returned to the hotel. His notices were out and his lectures announced almost before we had arrived.

At lunch I met him in the company of several ladies, among them one who was already old, with completely white hair, and who possessed features of a rare distinction. Mr. Train introduced her to me: "Mrs. Elizabeth Cady Stanton," he said. I bowed. I already knew Mrs. Stanton by name as one of the great promoters of the emancipation of women in the United States, and I was happy to meet her in person.[2]

[1] The same whose arrest in Ireland in January of 1868 was to cause such a stir. [*Simonin's note.*]

George Francis Train was indeed a controversial figure. American born, he was a member of the Fenians, a secret order founded in New York in 1856 and dedicated to the overthrow of English rule in Ireland. Train, known as an eccentric, lectured in America, England, and Ireland on Irish independence and women's rights.

[2] Elizabeth Cady Stanton (1815–1902), the wife of Henry B. Stanton, journalist and abolitionist, was a prominent leader of the women's rights movement.

The Emancipation of Women

When I say emancipation of women, you will understand that I use the word in the most moral and most elevated sense. Madam Stanton asks that women enjoy the same rights as men, and has founded an association for this goal, the Equal Rights Association, much talked of.

Madam Stanton has overlooked nothing to arrive at her goal; she has given all, her time, her fortune; and today, out of her private funds and her own labor, she supports all the proceedings, the publications, and the activities of the great association. She is even talking of founding a journal in New York to be devoted to the defense of the sacred cause, namely, the emancipation of women.[3]

When I had the honor of meeting her in Omaha, Madam Stanton had just returned from a long campaign in Kansas with her worthy and tireless lieutenant, Miss Susan Anthony, at the same time her secretary.[4] In Kansas they had converted a goodly number of women to the new theory, and not a few men. Among the latter, Madam Stanton cited with pleasure the name of the present governor of Kansas.

Mr. Francis Train has for some time made himself an advocate of the feminine cause. He is one of the most famous lecturers in the United States, and, when I met him in Cheyenne, was just returning from a tour of Colorado and the Rocky Mountains, where he had all in one breath given lectures, improvised verses in public, approved a big hotel in Cheyenne and a branch of the railroad toward Denver, and hunted buffalo with his young daughter, who, in her turn, had killed several of these wild animals. So things go in America, and no one thinks the worse of it.

The Association for Equal Rights could not pass up Mr. Train, the most active man in the United States, "the fastest man in America," as he is called, without making sure of this powerful recruit. The great agitator quickly consented to add this new string to his bow, and soon he was called only the Woman's Advocate. All his other titles, even that of "the people's man," paled before this one.

"Can you speak in Omaha November 19, in Des Moines the 21st, in

[3] She has since put this project into execution by founding a weekly sheet entitled *The Revolution*. [*Simonin's note.*]

[4] Susan B. Anthony (1820–1906) was a militant agitator for woman and Negro suffrage, temperance, and women's civil rights. Working closely with Mrs. Stanton, she was co-editor of *The Revolution*.

145

Chicago the 22nd, in Milwaukee the 23rd, in St. Louis the 26th, in Louisville the 27th, in Cincinnati the 28th, in Cleveland the 29th, in Albany the 4th, in Springfield the 6th, in Worcester the 7th, in Boston the 9th, in Hartford the 10th, in Philadelphia the 12th, in New York the 14th? Say yes, and the women will be with you! Long live rights!"

Such was the telegram which the leading members of the Association for Equal Rights sent him recently, signed by Mesdames or Misses Stenny, W. A. Starret, A. Robinson [*sic*], Sarah Brown, Lucy Stone, Olympia Brown, E. C. Stanton, S. Anthony.[5] To whom Mr. Train immediately parried with this telegram: "To the women composing the committee on votes for women: Yes! and may God protect the right, and have pity on the souls of those who refuse to give the vote to women! Signed: G. F. Train."

After all, what did this amount to for so intrepid a warrior? To give eighteen lectures in twenty-five days, and to cover I do not know how many hundreds of miles on the American railroads, to run about a country as vast as half of Europe and to stop and speak in eighteen large cities. Does not one sleep on the railroad in the United States? Does not one rest on Sunday? "I once did better than that," said Mr. Train to me the other day; "I made thirty talks in twelve days."

He gave two lectures the day we were in Omaha, that is, two meetings of two hours each, on the same day, one in the afternoon, one in the evening. I heard him talk, too, in Cheyenne one evening at nine o'clock, in full moonlight, in the public square, before the rude pioneers of the Far West. He had climbed on a box without more ceremony, while the mayor of Cheyenne, who had introduced him to the public, crouched at his feet. The orator could have done without the introduction in a pinch, for everyone in the United States knows him.

---

5 Stenny is probably an error for Mrs. R. S. Tenny, a Lawrence, Kansas, physician; or it could refer to Sarah Brownson, the daughter of the well-known clergyman and reformer Orestes A. Brownson, who married William J. Tenny. Mrs. Helen Ekin Starret, whose husband was a clergyman and regent and secretary of the University of Kansas; Mrs. Harriet H. Robinson, wife of the Boston editor William S. Robinson; Sarah A. Brown of Kansas, who was to become the first woman in the United States to be nominated for a state office by a leading political party; Lucy Stone of Massachusetts, who later helped organize the American Woman's Suffrage Association; and the Reverend Olympia Brown, an ordained Universalist minister from Massachusetts, were all active in the women's rights movement. See Elizabeth Cady Stanton, *History of Woman Suffrage* (3 vols.; New York: Fowler and Wells, 1881).

The Emancipation of Women

Mr. Train talks about everything in his lectures, himself first of all, about politics and politicians, the Pacific railroad, temperance societies, the next presidential election, for which he openly proposes himself as a candidate, and finally on the right of women to the suffrage. He must have begun his lecture in Omaha with this latter topic. Actually, the public does not share his ideas on this subject.

As is customary in the United States, Mr. Train puts questions to his listeners: "Do you want your wives, your daughters, your sisters, to have fewer political rights than the negroes?" And a significant growl indicates that the audience, composed almost entirely of men, is not at all inclined to grant women the right of suffrage. Mr. Train twice put it to the test, with the same failure. He had succeeded no better before this at Cheyenne, for everywhere the audience seemed to be telling him that in its opinion women were perfect if

> Capacity of mind no higher rose
> Than tell a jacket from the nether clothes.

Madam Stanton followed Mr. Train. I have rarely seen a nobler, more dignified woman. She is past sixty years of age; her features, as I have said, are unusually distinguished. Her thick, white hair, naturally curly, is combed with the greatest care. She wore that day a black silk dress with a high collar held together at the neck with an exceptionally fine cameo. Miss S. Anthony was likewise in black. She has passed her fortieth year and wears spectacles, and feature for feature recalls that type of tall, thin English traveler whom we so often see in Paris.

I have dwelt on the costumes of these women to show that in America one may defend political suffrage for women and demand the same rights as for men without wearing pantalettes, a raincoat, a pointed hat, and a necktie, as the "bloomers" did. However, the masculine costume has been adopted, I am told, by some of the most advanced partisans of the cause so worthily led by Mesdames Stanton and Anthony.

Madam Stanton gave an hour's lecture at Omaha. She spoke standing, without notes, leaning her hand on a table and looking directly at her audience, though without the slightest trace of brazenness, but with much dignity and self-respect. She spoke slowly, and demanded one by one the same rights for women as for men, not only political but also civil rights. She asked for married women the right to carry on a business and to inherit like the husband, things the laws of the United States do not everywhere permit. She demonstrated by numerous examples (and might have cited herself as one) that woman is in no respect inferior to man. She named from history Joan of Arc, Marie Thérèse, and many others; and in American literature, Miss Harriet Beecher Stowe, author of *Uncle Tom's Cabin*; in French literature, George Sand, and so on. Among the most convinced supporters of the ideas which she defended she recalled various well-known names, among others, that of John Stuart Mill, the great English economist.

The audience applauded on several occasions, but it was clear that it was not convinced, or, if you wish, converted to the opinions of the speaker, even in the feminine portion. Miss Anthony, who followed Madam Stanton, was no more successful in winning her listeners.

I accompanied Mr. Train and these two ladies from Omaha to Chicago, and on the way became more fully acquainted with Madam Stanton. We talked of Paris. She knows our literature well, and even spent some time in Paris, a few years ago. The special subject of conversation was always the question of the emancipation of women. There are already women doctors, perhaps lawyers, in the United States; and indeed they have a role there. A few are ministers of the gospel. Madam Stanton has presented her name for the legislature of New York. And indeed, she would fill the position, even in the federal Congress, better than many a deputy with none too good a reputation with the public.

"Imagine a woman consul," some ill-willed joker said to her. "You go to get your passport visa signed and you are told, 'Madame is giving birth to a child!'"

"In that case, address yourself to the chief official," she replied. "Isn't that the answer you get when the consul is ill or has spent the night gambling or elsewhere?"

It is impossible to predict yet what the outcome will be of this question of the political emancipation of women.[6] New ideas propagate

[6] Two years later, in 1869, Wyoming Territory granted woman suffrage, the first state or territory in the United States to do so. In 1870 Laramie witnessed the first woman jury in United States history.

so rapidly in this country, and move so swiftly from theory to practice, that what is regarded as an error the day before becomes a truth tomorrow. Do we not already see mixed colleges in the northern states, where young men and young women study Latin, Greek, and mathematics together, and where the young women often surpass the boys? All is dared in America, and the results justify so much boldness.

Do I hear you say that it is only a matter of climate? It is more. It is a question of freedom well understood. "Help yourself," says the American; tend to your own affairs yourself.

I return to the specific question which we have been discussing, that of granting women all the rights that men enjoy. I am forced to recognize that this question has as yet made no great progress in the United States, except perhaps in Kansas and Massachusetts. "Why?" you ask. "Has it not been clearly enough defined, well enough presented?"

You have seen what skillful and eloquent advocates have undertaken to defend it. I suspect that Mr. Dixon[7] was right in his examination of this subject in his book, *New America*, when he quoted the cry of a young Bostonian woman: "Well, afterwards, when we have the same rights as men, no one will bother further about us. That is why we don't want it." The question is still pending; it is, as you have seen, far from being resolved, and we must grant the future the burden of saying the last word on a subject as delicate as that of the emancipation of women.

[7] This is probably James Dixon (1814–1873), a Connecticut lawyer and Whig, United States Senator from 1857 to 1863. He dabbled in poetry and belles-lettres.

CHAPTER 20

The Empire City

New York, 27 November

New York, where I have just arrived, has grown even since I last passed through. It is indeed the Empire City, as the Americans call it with a legitimate pride. Scarcely two hundred and fifty years ago Manhattan Island was bought for a few shillings by the Hollanders, the first colonizers in the area, from the Indians who inhabited the region. Here the Hollanders laid the foundations for New Amsterdam, which the English later called New York. Today the island of Manhattan has become too narrow for the growth of the great city, which encompasses almost a million and a half inhabitants; and opposite it, all along the arm of the sea which is called the East River and along the Hudson, prosperous cities arise: Brooklyn, which has nearly 400,000 inhabitants, and Jersey City, which has more than 60,000.

To understand clearly not only the present progress but even their whole importance, you must note the location of these three cities on the map. Brooklyn and Jersey City are, in fact, two satellites of New York. They revolve around it and play their daily part in the advancement of the great metropolis, which alone will count several million inhabitants before the end of the century, for here the population doubles every fifteen years.

New York is situated on a broad bay, better protected and no less beautiful than the boasted bay of Naples. A narrow inlet protects it against the winds and waves of the open sea. Never a sheet of water

150

offered a spectacle quite like it: steamboats and sailing vessels pass back and forth in veritable fleets. On the other side of the bay descends one of the most magnificent rivers in the world, the Hudson. All kinds of vessels anchor freely on its banks, which are framed by perpendicular bluffs above the water, forming the safest of natural ports, since at their surface these bluffs are level with the ground; and at the center of the river's deep waters vessels of the greatest tonnage can ascend as far as Albany, the capital of the state and 135 miles from New York. The landscape is ravishing all along the passage. Here the "Pallisades," an enormous lava flow reaching to a height of 500 feet, stretch along the right bank of the river like a veritable fortification; there the green hills of West Point and the blue mountains of the Catskills dominate the windings of the river, where it suddenly widens,[1] so that you would think yourself in the midst of one of the Swiss lakes. The Americans are proud of their beautiful river. The first question they ask the newly debarked traveler is "Have you sailed on the Hudson?"

Immense steamers, truly floating hotels, decorated with a luxury of which we have no conception in France, ascend and descend the Hudson at all times. Soft carpets are stretched everywhere in vast salons of gilded paneling. Tables and seats of artistic form further adorn the interior of the ship. No greater pains would be taken in France for a king on a voyage. Here everybody is the king: he is the people, and everywhere he is spoiled and pampered. Young misses, laughing and flirting, and gentlemen, quieter, press in crowds into the salons or about the outer decks while the vessel advances at full steam. If a competitor is following the same route, a contest of speed often takes place to see who will arrive first. A captain one day, in a contest of the sort, found himself out of fuel, for in order to double the speed, eight times the amount of coal has to be consumed; the machine determines that. Now our captain wanted to win at all costs. He threw all the furniture of his ship into the furnace, and then, as the pressure of the steam increased beyond safety, he seated himself bravely on the safety valve, crying to the engineers, "Come on, boys, one last effort!" If the boiler had exploded, the passengers would certainly have gone up

[1] The Tappan Zee.

with it, but they applauded the captain and thought of one thing only, to be the first to arrive. So goes the world in America. A concern for security hardly exists here on a voyage, but they travel nonetheless and generally arrive. So much the worse for those who get in the way! That is one of those misfortunes to be encountered in the battle of life. This indifference to danger on the part of Americans constitutes an element of their strength and reveals the secret of the astonishing results they achieve in their vast colonization.

I return to the Empire City. Will you disembark with me? Our steamer has just touched the wharf. The outskirts of the commercial city are hardly attractive, and the streets are everywhere badly paved, dirty, and full of holes, especially in winter. In a free, democratic system, the weakness is that the task of doing everything is left to everyone, whereas with us all is well done under a strongly centralized system. The New York municipality concerns itself little with the city and lets things go in proportion. We pass before a market which is a muddy charnel house, such as the dirtiest hamlet in France would reject. Now we are in Wall, Pearl, and Beaver streets. What activity! What movement! It surpasses the city of London itself. Heavy wagons come and go, laden with all the merchandise of the globe: bales of cotton or wool, sacks of coffee, chests of tea, casks of sugar or tobacco, barrels of wine or petroleum. The waggoner, upright on his vehicle like an ancient conqueror, whips his horses vigorously and shouts to passers-by who do not get out of his way quickly enough. At right and left are the offices of trade. On the ground floor are the changers, the exchange brokers, who traffic in stocks and shares and speculate in paper money, the only kind in circulation since the War of Secession. On the mezzanine and upper floors, bankers, shipowners, brokers, traders. Aside from a few offices fairly appropriately furnished, the offices are regular closets, holes, as, for that matter, they are in London, Manchester, Birmingham, Liverpool. In America, as in England, one has his office and his home. The office is in a section noisy with business; the home is in the most distant and quietest part of the city. Everyone comes freely into the office, even the newcomer, whoever he may be; in the house is the respected hearth, the "home." There one receives only his friends, chosen even in this democratic country with scrupulous care, for equality exists only on the surface and is no more absolute than elsewhere. The human heart is the same everywhere, and there is no perfect system of government.

Would you like to visit one of these offices? We are in Wall Street, pre-eminently the street of bankers and brokers. At the doors of each establishment are hung immense boards of black wood, divided into as many compartments as there are floors, and as many numbers as there are occupied cells. Before each number is inscribed in gold letters the name of the occupant or occupants, for the cost of rent is so high that sometimes several persons carry on their business in the same room—a touching confraternity. Office furniture is crude: wicker chairs, tables of the most common wood, a reserved enclosure which a broom rarely sees, and here and there enormous spittoons (excuse the word) in crude earthenware or rubber and shaped like a dish for potpie. Everybody "chews" in America, even in high places, and the "spittoon" has become an indispensable adjunct to the furnishings of every good Yankee.

Enter this office with me. I have a letter recommending me to the top official, a great banker of the country. I pronounce his name as I enter. A "gentleman," hat on his head, feet on the mantel of the fireplace, body ensconced in his "rocking-chair," holds out a hand to take the letter, and with the other hand gives his hat a shove to fix it more firmly in place. He reads the letter and returns it. "It's for my brother," he says, without in the least discommoding himself. "He will be very sorry not to have seen you. He is at present in Boston." And pulling a plug of tobacco from his pocket, he cuts off the customary amount with his knife, receives it in the hollow of his hand, and, with a well executed gesture, throws it with a single motion into his mouth. Then, passing me the knife and plug, he says, "Do you use it? Don't stand on ceremony."

"Thank you, I do not chew. Good day."

"Good-by."

I shall never see him again in my life, or his brother. With this offhand manner business is carried on everywhere.

The word *office*, which Americans and English apply to their *bureaux*, gave rise one day to a curious misunderstanding on the part of one of my friends who spoke very little English. Like me, he had a letter for an American businessman. Instead of taking it to the business office of the recipient, he presented himself one morning at his home. The servant replied, "Mr. X. is at his office."

"And until what time?" asked the traveler.

"Until three o'clock."

"A truly devout man," said my friend as he left; "then I shall return this evening." [2]

The more poorly kept and badly situated the office is, the more comfortable and cared for is the "home," established in the best section of the city. Each has his own house and occupies it alone. I do not know where all these people earn so much money that every one of them can pay for a house which unfurnished costs at least five hundred thousand francs, but the fact is there and I record it. And what comfort! Water on every floor, hot and cold, bathrooms, hot-air heating. The kitchen is confined to the basement by a separate stairway. Often a little garden, a flowering tree before the house, beside fine stone steps. All these dwellings, especially on Fifth Avenue, the most fashionable quarter and the most sumptuous, form magnificent rows, and we must admit that civil architecture is here well advanced. "But they are cardboard houses; these stones, so beautifully hewn and carved, are but veneer, false fronts," said one of those Frenchmen (and they are numerous) who find everything wrong in America. But what difference, if the lines are pure, graceful, and elegant, and if the house is comfortable, especially if the interior is conveniently arranged?

In some of these dwellings a luxury reigns which might be called princely. People with several millions of income are not rare in New York; and American merchants, like those of ancient Phoenicia, have the expense accounts of kings. Paintings, sculptures, art objects, the most elegant furnishings, the most renowned works of ancient and modern masters are literally heaped in some of these residences, and splendid entertainments are given in winter. Often all this is done without a great deal of taste—but let that pass; progress will come. "We are a young people; we need to learn. That is why we go to Europe." Many Americans answer this way when they meet you; they freely allow you

[2] In French, *à l'office* means at one's prayers or worship.

to criticize their country. Already the trips to Europe, which all of them make frequently, may be said to have been most profitable for them.

We welcome a whole colony of Americans every winter in Paris. You have seen them, have you not, those young *misses* with their wealth of hair, their lively eyes, their cheeks sometimes rosy, sometimes a bit pale, those *misses* with their well-formed, slender height, the dancers, the indefatigable talkers, every winter in Paris at all the *soirées*, and especially at the parties given by General Dix, who represents the American government with such dignity.[3] These fashionable young ladies have conquered all our young men, and more than one has never returned to her native land. Those who do return bring to New York their portion of good manners and new ideas, and by means of these dainty messengers American society progresses astonishingly. "Women count more than men with us," is the general cry in the United States. Too busy, too early removed from school life and the family, the men have not had time to give attention to their manners. But are not women everywhere the first and best teachers of men? Happy the land where their influence still prevails!

How much livelier and more graceful these young Americans are than the daughters of Albion. I ask the pardon of English women, but the American young women are the peer of the French (everywhere proclaimed without equal) for grace and spirit and the manner of wearing a dress. And how superior American beauty is to English! It possesses I know not what of greater strength, more energy, and a kind of frankness which does not offend. How many pretty women one meets when one strolls on Broadway at the hour when the crowds throng these boulevards of New York. "How could it be otherwise?" said an observant fellow to me yesterday. "In the first place, consider all these men who come here or who have come here, and from whom all these young women you so admire have sprung. Did they not come from all the lands of earth: English, German, Spanish of America, Scandinavians, Italians, French? Well, the mingling of such races cannot

[3] General John Adams Dix (1798–1879), onetime senator from New York, minister to France, Secretary of the Treasury under President Buchanan, and major general of New York state forces and volunteers, was again sent to France as minister in 1866. He was the first president of the Union Pacific Railroad and later became governor of New York.

help but yield some very fine products. Furthermore, every man who comes to the United States has something to him. Apart from some rare exceptions, he is neither an idler nor an ignoramus nor a delicate, sickly creature. He is enterprising, courageous; he has, as they say, a good foot, a good eye. Mating among such human beings has every chance of success."

I let my companion talk as we went down Broadway, and I concluded that he was right.

Shall I describe now that unusual street, more than four and a half miles long, which has been compared to the boulevards of Paris, but which is far from equaling them in the refinement of the shops or the spaciousness of the street, even if it surpasses them in certain aspects by the animation, and I know not what of that vivacity, even turbulence, the noise, the feverishness, which the American exhibits everywhere? Shall I describe the immense stores to be encountered all along Broadway, some of them unique in the world? Shall I depict the spectacle which this street offers at certain hours of the day? But all that has been twenty times said, and you know it by heart. You know, too, the churches, the theatres, the hotels, the squares, the park of the great city, its beautiful aqueduct, and all the public and private monuments, some of them well deserving attention. All that has been twenty times depicted, and I am not writing you to retell what others have said before me, or what may be found in all the travel guides and in all the geographical treatises.

CHAPTER 21

The American People

The end crowns the work. I leave for Europe, and shall see you in a dozen days in Paris. You will treat my voyage as telescoped, as fantastic. Others will say that I did not leave, but merely hid myself somewhere for three months. Three months! Indeed, that is all I needed to cover five thousand leagues [some twelve thousand miles], going and coming. Thanks to. steam, we are permitted to make such voyages, which you may rightly describe as telescoped, for it would formerly have required more than a year to accomplish such a trip, and God knows at the price of what fatigues and what dangers.

How much I have seen during these three months: the Pacific railroad, the pioneers of Colorado, the last Redskins! Yes, our voyage has been fantastic, but we shall have claimed the feeble merit only of having shown the way to our successors. It is up to you now to follow us, young compatriots who wish to see and, by your study of these new regions, to complete your somewhat too theoretical education in your native land.

Freedom and work, and let us not forget it, alone made possible the creation of all these marvels which we have admired. The American people, in whom are summed up these two things, freedom and work, have the undeniable merit of practicing them everywhere and at all times. The American people are the whole world, Europe as well as America. Every year Europe sends three hundred thousand of her children to the United States, and the strongest and most vigorous, the producers and reproducers, as an economist has called them. Whereas among us young men are regimented for the destructive exercises of war, there they are taken for the productive labors of peace. Do you perceive the difference? Our young men from the country areas, when they return from their military service, become negative values; they are worth less than nothing because they have been taught to destroy. The young men who emigrate to the United States are, on the contrary, positive values because they have been taught to create. And do you know their value? They are valued at a thousand dollars apiece, 5,000 francs. This is the fictive price which one emigrant is assumed to be worth here as soon as he sets foot on the shores of the Union.

In all that there is of good, let us try to imitate the American people who form today, as it were, a synthesis of all other peoples. Let us practice work and freedom, like them. Do you believe that we would be no longer capable of founding colonies if we had fewer administrative controls and more liberal institutions?

You know how difficult it is in our colonies, in Algeria, for example, to become a landowner, how the obtainment there of any grant of land is surrounded with many long, vexing formalities. You know what happens, on the contrary, in the Far West. The firstcomer there may occupy 160 acres (64 hectares) of virgin land in a territory. He does not even need to be an American. Even if he debarked the day before in the United States, it is assumed that he has the intention (this is verbatim) of becoming a citizen of the great republic, and that is all. He pays a certain sum at the land office (around fifteen francs per hectare— a dollar an acre), and there he is, permanently set up as a landed proprietor. Such are the liberal measures which have brought prosperity to the distant territories of the Union.

You will remind me that the land here belongs to no one, that the space is immense, and that everywhere one could, as they say, cut out of whole cloth. I reply that in most of our colonies, where the same conditions are present, we have never reached the marvelous success of the American pioneers. Why? Because the administrative measures so stubbornly adopted by us have never been inspired by anything except narrow, suspicious, and extortionate ideas; because centralization with us kills all, and the colonies, even the most distant, cannot act without receiving the password from the metropolis. And what a contrast! Among our colonists, indolence, uncertainty, failure; among the Americans, eagerness, feverish activity, the most amazing success.

Do not tell me again that in Algeria we have the Arabs, with whom we must come to terms or fight. The pioneers of the Far West have also the Redskins, their Bedouins, and you know that these have often caused them much trouble.

It is by liberty, not by authoritative measures, that colonies are founded, and the American people offer us a fine example to imitate. If I brought back no more than this lesson from my whole voyage, to know that all latitude must be given to personal initiative, especially liberty of action, my journey, however brief, would have been one of the most profitable.

But I have also learned to esteem and to love even more warmly a great people whom I had already known; I have better understood its institutions, the most liberal, the most democratic that men have ever known. My voyage will thus have been of service to me in all ways, and I recommend to tourists on vacation this means, henceforth at their disposal, of profiting by their summer's leisure. Let them take the route to New York instead of to Baden, and the way to the Rocky Mountains instead of to the Alps. The scenery will be as fine, and the profit certainly greater.

We shall speak further of all this, for I wish to return here next year for a longer journey. I should like, before the Pacific railroad is completed, to cover all the great desert to the ocean, to salute my friends the Mormons, to inspect the work of the miners of the silver veins in Nevada, as I have those of the Rocky Mountains, and finally to visit again beautiful, fertile California, which I have not visited since seven years ago. I shall do all that, and I may return even a further time, for one grows attached to this country and appreciates it the more one studies it. As for today, I am steering for Brest. In a dozen days I shall be in Paris; and I conclude by saying, like Cicero to Atticus, *Vale!* Farewell, or, if you prefer, *Au revoir!*

Appendix:

Newspaper Accounts of Simonin's Trip

In various publications of the time we may follow Simonin's progress through the West, and in addition see the reactions of the Americans whom he met during his travels.

In a long letter dated August 12, 1867, in the September 19 *Daily Miners' Register* of Central City, Colorado Territory, Mr. Whitney, writing from Paris, announced that "Monsieur L. Simonin, an engineer and mineralogist of much reputation in scientific circles here, and connected with the Central School of Mines, is preparing to leave for Colorado under government direction to report on the mineral interests of the territory." Colonel Heine, he adds, "a German engineer of reputation, at present attached to the American legation in Paris," has also promised to visit Central City.

Mr. Whitney goes on to stress the value of the American exhibit at the Paris Exposition, and notes that he has distributed eight thousand pamphlets, in three languages, on mining activities. He adds that there is no danger of European claims to possessions in the West—a reference perhaps to Colonel Heine's interest in German settlements along the new Union Pacific line.

The *American Journal of Mining*, published in New York City, reported on September 28, 1867 (Vol. IV, No. 13, n. s.), the arrival of M. Simonier [*sic*], "a distinguished geologist and mineralogist," and professor of mineralogy at the Ecoles des Mines. Mr. Whitney, returning with him, is said to be organizing a large company in Paris with a capital of ten million francs, with the object of smelting Colorado ores, and a similar company in London. The problem, says the *Journal*, is still that of saving a large percentage of the metal from the crude ore. Yet European methods are being studied, and ingenious American inventions are appearing.

The Central City *Daily Miners' Register* said on October 8: "Mr. Whitney, accompanied by M. Simone [*sic*] and Col. Heine, arrived here from Boulder on Sunday. . . . The results of their observations will be published in the Paris *Moniteur* and other leading journals in Europe. Their reports will doubtless have a great influence on emigration and the direction of capital here."

About M. Simonin's lecture to the Central City miners, the *American Journal of Mining* for November 16, 1867 (Vol. IV, No. 20, n. s.), carried this item in an editorial: "The lecturer is said to have spoken English with such a broken accent that it was difficult to follow him, yet we should think, from the reports in the newspapers that he succeeded in delivering an interesting address." Although there was not much in it "new or particularly valuable," one could not expect a visitor to learn a great deal in five days.

"In some respects," the editorial continues, "Europeans are less acquainted with the occurrence and treatment of gold than we are. . . . If M. Simonin were as well acquainted with American ores as he is with history, he would not have said that 'silver never occurs like gold in alluvial deposits.' . . . We find," the editorial adds, "one golden paragraph"; this is to the effect that there is a distinction between chemistry and metallurgy: the chemist works in a laboratory, while the metallurgist must know not only how to extract metals, but how to calculate whether it will pay to extract them in a certain manner. Chemistry plays an important part, but it must not take the place of metallurgy.

The *Rocky Mountain News* of October 31 reported that "Colonel Heine and Prof. Simonin arrived in town last evening," on their return from Georgetown and Central City.

On November 2, the Cheyenne *Leader* ran the following:

Prof. Simonin and Col. Heine called upon us, on their way from the mines of Colorado to the grand peace council at [Fort] Laramie—

perhaps the last Indian council, as the Col. expressed it. These distinguished gentlemen have devoted several weeks in exploring the mining regions, and in thoroughly examining the gold and silver bearing ores. They have presented the results of their observations in several scientific lectures before the Miners and Mechanics institute, in Central City, to the great delight and gratification of the mining people. They express great confidence in the ultimate success of the Colorado mines .... We do not think they were duly impressed with the skill of American mining; and [we think] that much more headway would be made, when mining and the reduction of ores were separated and carried on as distinctive branches, as much so as producing wheat and manufacturing flour. Professor Simonin is a correspondent of the Paris *Moniteur*, and is represented as a gentleman of the highest scientific attainments. Col. Heine's post of duty is at Paris, and he now has leave of absence for nineteen days for this visit.

The November 7 *Leader* said: "OFF FOR LARAMIE. Col. Heine, Mons. Simonin, and Mr. Hines, correspondent of the Chicago *Times*, left yesterday noon for Fort Laramie, to attend the peace council with the Indians at that point."

On November 19, the Cheyenne *Leader* reported:

Col. Heine and Prof. Simonin have just returned from the Council at Laramie. Several chiefs, of the Crows and Arapahoes were in attendance. The Sioux failed to come in, but are expected at North Platte, whither the Commissioners proceed to make another effort. The first named tribes were very friendly, and were willing to go on reservations, and the Crows will sign a treaty as soon as the Sioux shall open the way.

An acquaintance of ours, who was a witness to the proceedings at Laramie, characterizes the whole affair as a miserable failure and barren of beneficial results. There were about three hundred Indians present of the tribes above named, with a few Cheyennes. General Harney did not regard them as at all worthy of forming a treaty with. The Commission virtually promised the Crows, and through them, the Sioux, to abandon the northern forts and roads, which seems to be their finality. He says that in almost every lodge, and he was in them all, he found a skulking white man.

Four chapters, 5–8, translated by Colonel Heine, ran in the Central City *Daily Miners' Register* for May 19 and June 9, 17, and 18, 1868.

Colonel Heine's translations are quite true to the original, although he occasionally tactfully softens a phrase. For example, "no cooks" in America becomes "few good cooks"; and the descriptions of the dark towels (Chapter 6) and the poor playing of the Central City band, as well as the paragraph that follows on the lectures, are omitted entirely.

The *Register* of May 16 reads: "Hon. J. P. Whitney sends us a letter written by Prof. Simonin and published in the Paris *Moniteur* of March 24th. The translation was made by Col. W. Heine. The letter abounds in compliments to Colorado and the enterprise of her people. The condition of the mines, with the Professor's scientific explanation of them, will appear in other letters to be published by us at an early date."

The May 17 *Register* said:

We are in receipt from the Hon. J. P. Whitney, of two numbers of *Le Tour du Monde*, a periodical published in Paris under the direction of Dr. M. Eduard Charton. It is near the size of Frank Leslie's Magazine, each containing letters, richly illustrated, from the glowing pen of Professor Simonin. The sketches are all from Colorado; and are executed with the highest skill, representing the city of Denver, a fine map of the Territory, and scenes on Monument Creek, Indian portraits, singly and grouped, maps of Gilpin and Clear Creek counties, the Garden of the Gods, Pike's Peak, Long's Peak, a Pilgrim whacking bulls across the continent, evidently a 59'er, an attack upon Wells Fargo & Co's coaches by the Indians, village of prairie dogs, discovery of twelve soldiers murdered by the Indians, camp life, etc., etc., all portrayed in the most artistic style. The Professor's description of these being in French, a language not spoken freely hereabouts, and of which we know as little as of Hindoo, is not immediately available, but Mr. Whitney has promised to do the translation and send it on for publication. Then we shall know all about it, and until then we ask you to wait.

Acknowledgements

I am indebted to Mr. Gene M. Gressley, archivist at the University of Wyoming, for suggesting a full translation of this little book, from which I had excerpted certain passages some years ago, and for his critical reading of the manuscript. Portions of the chapters on Cheyenne and Fort Laramie appeared previously in my translation in the *Frontier* magazine, X (1930) and XI (1931); and certain parts on Colorado in 1867 were published in the *Colorado Magazine,* XIV (1937), though these pages have been retranslated here.

I wish also to thank the staffs of the University of Wyoming Library, and of the Western section of the Denver Public Library, and the Wyoming State Archives, for their never failing courtesies and helpfulness.

WILSON O. CLOUGH

Index

167

Index

169